Text to Note
Study Skills for Advanced Learners

Alex Adkins and Ian McKean

Edward Arnold

©Alex Adkins and Ian McKean 1983

First published 1983
by Edward Arnold (Publishers) Ltd
41 Bedford Square, London WC1B 3DQ

British Library Cataloguing in Publication Data.

Adkins, Alex
    Text to note: study skills for advanced learners.
    1. Note-taking — Problems, exercises, etc.
    I. Title   II. McKean, Ian
    808'.066   LB1049

ISBN 0-7131-8077-3

All Rights Reserved.
No part of this publication may be reproduced, stored in a retrieval system, or transmitted in any form or by any means, electronic, mechanical, photocopying, recording or otherwise, without the prior permission of Edward Arnold (Publishers) Ltd.

Set in 10/11pt IBM Press Roman by The Castlefield Press of Northampton
Printed in Great Britain by Thomson Litho Ltd, East Kilbride

Contents

		Page
Introduction		v
Unit 1	Using Your Dictionary	1
Unit 2	Note-making	8
Unit 3	Earthquakes	17
Unit 4	Energy Sources	22
Unit 5	The Whale	26
Unit 6	Silicon Chips	31
Unit 7	Rubber	37
Unit 8	Volcanoes	41
Unit 9	Function	48
Unit 10	Kalahari Bushmen	53
Unit 11	The Camera	58
Unit 12	Pliny and Pompeii	65
Unit 13	Lasers and Holograms	71
Unit 14	Sleep and Dreams	77
Unit 15	The World's Weather	82
Unit 16	Heat Control & The Skin	89
Unit 17	Computers	92
Unit 18	Arthritis	96
Unit 19	The World's Food	100
Unit 20	The Cinema	103
Tapescript		106

Introduction

What this course is

Text to Note is a course for those who are studying or intend to study another subject through the medium of English. It concentrates on the following skills needed for study.
1. Understanding and interpreting written texts and non-verbal information such as charts, diagrams, graphs and flow charts.
2. Understanding short lectures on subjects related to the reading texts.
3. Making notes based on the reading and the lectures.
4. Using these notes to perform a range of tasks.

It also gives opportunities for discussion both about the completed tasks and the topics on which the units are based.

Text to Note is intended to encourage the learner to become increasingly independent in using the techniques of study. Some of the support given in earlier units (especially in note-making) is later taken away and, although the book is not structurally graded, there is an overall increase in the difficulty of the texts and tasks.

Who it is for

The course is for learners whose English is at or above upper-intermediate level (the level of the Cambridge First Certificate in English) and who need either to learn the skills of study or to learn how to use familiar skills in the unfamiliar medium of English, either in Britain or elsewhere.

It is suitable for those about to begin or already engaged in courses in further and higher education and also for students preparing to take the JMB — the Joint Matriculation Board's Test in English (Overseas).

What it contains

Text to Note does not aim to teach any subject or subjects as such. It is organized around a variety of topics, chosen to be of interest to a wide range of people.

Certain patterns of thinking, speaking and writing are typical in many areas of study. Among the most common are:
1. Description.
2. Sequencing: describing processes; giving instructions; narrating events.
3. Comparison.
4. Classification.
5. Cause and effect.

Each unit involves one or more of these patterns. Most contain more than one. The language needed for expressing each of these cognitive operations often shows certain typical markers and structures (for instance, 'first', 'then', 'after that' are common sequence markers; a sentence pattern such as 'While . . . , on the other hand . . .' is normally used to contrast two points).

The talks are recorded on cassette; the tapescript is on pages 106–119.

Units 1 and 2 These are introductory units to encourage the effective use of monolingual dictionaries (especially learners' dictionaries) and to introduce the basic skill of making notes. Unit 2 (Note-making) is designed to provide continuing support to the student, who should refer to it throughout the course.

Unit 3 — 15 Each of these begins with a reading passage on a particular topic, followed by exercises to develop understanding and tasks based on the information given. For certain exercises, locations in the reading passage are indicated by paragraph and then by the line within it. The purpose of this is to encourage the learner to appreciate the role of the paragraph as a unit in written discourse.

There is then a short lecture on the same or a closely related topic. The lecture is usually in three parts and is accompanied by note-making exercises. Further tasks follow, some related specifically to the lecture, others depending on an understanding of both the reading passage and the lecture.

Units 16 — 20 The main differences in these units are:
1. The lecture is at the beginning. A very brief outline of its content is given but no further assistance is offered. In this way, the note-making task moves closer to the learning context the student will meet beyond the language class.
2. The reading passages are from authentic sources and are thus more unpredictable in style and difficulty.

Types of activity

Reading
1. Pre-read (Units 3–15)
   The purpose of this is to direct the student's attention to the topic, thereby stimulating interest and establishing existing knowledge.
2. Content Skim (Units 3–20)
   This is the first exercise to follow the reading passage. Its form varies but it is always intended to develop an overall grasp of the passage, its structure and the key points within it. It also serves to develop the skill of reading at speed.
3. Comprehension Scan (Units 3–20)
   This encourages a more detailed appreciation of the text. In some cases it concentrates entirely on direct content judgments (especially of the true/false/insufficient evidence type); in others it aims to develop understanding above sentence level by asking the student to supply the references of pronouns or identify the significance of certain discourse markers.

Listening
4. Decoding (Units 3–15)
   One of the problems faced by a non-native speaker when listening to a talk or lecture is that of actually identifying what is being said. This is particularly true of English, where weak forms and contractions are very frequent in the structural parts of the language. Effective understanding depends both on knowledge of what *could* be said and on familiarity with the phonological patterns of connected speech. The gap-filling exercises which accompany Part 1 of these lectures are to help the student in this area of difficulty. They concentrate on the recognition of structural elements but also include certain key lexical items, primarily to reinforce grasp of sound-spelling correspondences. Initial decoding exercises are provided in Unit 1.
5. Controlled Note-making (Units 3–15)
   In this type of exercise, an outline of the notes is provided, following the general pattern set out in the unit on note-making (Unit 2). The notes are

then completed during the relevant part of the lecture.
6. Guided Note-making (Units 3–15)
Here, only headings are given for the notes and the student must then make decisions as to what and how much to write.
7. Free Note-making (Units 16–20)
No framework is given for the notes on each lecture and the student is entirely responsible for the form and content of his or her notes.

Note   In all cases it is very important that the students have time, before hearing each part of the lecture, to read through the incomplete notes to make sure that they understand what is given. Before completing the decoding exercise, they should try to anticipate, from their knowledge of English, what some of the gap-fillers are likely to be. Also, they will very probably need to hear each section of the lecture more than once. In later units they might be allowed to hear the lecture only once but then, after each part, ask the teacher for information they did not gather. The teacher, in the role of lecturer, would then repeat the required information, preferably in a slightly different form but, of course, with identical content.

Tasks   These complete each unit by giving the students opportunities to practise their skills through fulfilling various tasks in relation to the topic of that unit. They are very varied in form and purpose but certain types recur:
classifying
identifying (often in the form of labelling)
describing
comparing/contrasting
defining
sequencing
following instructions
writing (this task heading is always used where a piece of continuous prose is required, regardless of the functions or operations involved)

A further note to the teacher

This is a skill-based, not a content-based course. The topics have been chosen to be of general interest and at a level which neither excludes those who know little about a particular subject nor insults those who do know about it. Technical terms, where used, are explained or their meanings are clear in context. It is, however, very important that you should be aware of cases where you need to provide support before, during or after a unit. This support may include the pre-teaching of lexical items (especially as a preparation for the lectures) and practice in the recognition and use of structural items and discourse markers. Some of these are indicated at the end of the book, but only you can know precisely the needs of your students.

Note that locations in the reading passages are indicated by paragraph and the line within it. Many students do not realise the importance or structured nature of the paragraph as a unit of meaning. By getting used to seeing paragraphs rather than sentences as the important building blocks in a text, they will learn to read and write more effectively.

The units may vary slightly in the amount of time needed to complete them satisfactorily. On average, two 2 hour sessions per unit should be sufficient. Writing tasks may be completed outside the classroom.

Study is largely a private activity but there are many opportunities in this book for students to work together. Note-making and other tasks should normally be completed by the student working independently, but checking and deciding on points about which there is disagreement may fruitfully be done in pairs, groups or by general discussion. Some topics may themselves generate debate or the desire for follow-up activities and these provide opportunities to practise speaking skills.

Students should be encouraged to use good monolingual learners' dictionaries. Unit 1 familiarises them with the basis for the effective use of these. When the students have done their best to deduce the meaning of an unfamiliar word from its context, they should feel free to refer to the dictionary.

A note to the student working alone

This course is designed with your needs in mind as well as those of students in class-based courses. This means that, wherever necessary, instructions are given clearly so you know what to do although there is no teacher to ask. The course gives you an opportunity to practise many of the skills you will need in order to study a subject in English. It does not contain traditional language exercises. Make sure you have a good dictionary, of the kind recommended in Unit 1, and a good grammar to refer to when your existing knowledge is not enough. You will need the cassette of the lectures and the tapescript that goes with it. Even without the cassette, however, there are parts of each unit (those based on the reading passage) that you can work with, but the cassette is really necessary if you want to get the best out of this course.

Tapescript

The tapescript of all the talks is at the end of this book.

Key

A Key with answers and suggested answers to the exercises in *Text to Note* is available separately.

Acknowledgements

The Publishers would like to thank the following for permission to reproduce copyright material:

The Arthritis and Rheumatism Council for the article 'My Research' by Dr Valerie E. Jones; P. Bishop for an extract from *Comprehensive Computer Studies* published by Edward Arnold; D. V. Hubbard for an extract from *Your Body/How it Works* published by Edward Arnold; Olympus Optical Co. (Europa) GmBH for extracts from the Olympus Trip 35 instruction booklet; Oxford University Press for extracts from A. S. Hornby (ed.) *Oxford Advanced Learner's Dictionary of Current English* and Thorold Dickinson *A Discovery of Cinema*; and D. & M. Pimental for an extract from *Food, Energy and Society*, 'Resource and Environmental Sciences' series published by Edward Arnold.

Unit 1   Using Your Dictionary

If you are serious about wanting to learn a language, it is essential that you get for yourself a good dictionary. A pocket dictionary is all right for quick reference when you are moving around and a bilingual dictionary can also be helpful. But you will be helped most to build up your vocabulary in English by studying definitions and explanations *in English*. Excellent dictionaries for the learner are available. They are compiled with your needs in mind and they give a great deal of information about the pronunciation, meaning and usage (grammar) of words and phrases.

In order to use your dictionary effectively, you should make yourself familiar with its apparatus — the system of symbols and abbreviations used in the entries. You will not all have the same dictionary, so this course cannot give you practice in using any particular one. On the other hand, it is possible in this unit to help you understand some of the features of the language better and to illustrate the information contained in a dictionary by giving an example. As you increase your understanding of the language and your skill in using a dictionary, you will feel greater confidence and learn better.

Listening and Pronunciation

In English, the relation between spelling and pronunciation is complicated, but there are clear patterns and rules. Whenever you look up a word in the dictionary, check the pronunciation, look at the word and say it several times. Most dictionaries use a form of the phonetic alphabet. Here are the symbols of the International Phonetic Alphabet and words to illustrate the sounds.

1. Look at the symbols while you listen to the tape and repeat the words.

vowels and diphthongs

/iː/	see	/ɜː/	fur	
/ɪ/	sit	/ə/	about, butt<u>er</u>fly, pap<u>er</u>	(the weak sound which
/e/	ten	/eɪ/	wage	is very common in
/æ/	hat	/əʊ/	home	unstressed syllables)
/ɑː/	arm	/aɪ/	time	
/ɒ/	not	/aʊ/	cow	
/ɔː/	saw	/ɔɪ/	boy	
/ʊ/	foot	/ɪə/	fear	
/uː/	do	/eə/	there	
/ʌ/	nut	/ʊə/	pure	

consonants

/p/	pat	/tʃ/	chip	/s/	sip	/n/	now
/b/	bat	/dʒ/	job	/z/	zip	/ŋ/	sing
/t/	tear	/f/	fan	/ʃ/	ship	/l/	load
/d/	dear	/v/	van	/ʒ/	vision	/r/	road
/k/	cold	/θ/	thick	/h/	hope	/j/	yes
/g/	gold	/ð/	that	/m/	man	/w/	was

A dictionary also shows which syllables of words are stressed. Here is one way of marking the main (primary) stress:

/ɪkˈsperɪmənt/ (experiment)

The vertical line indicates that this word is stressed on the second syllable: exp<u>e</u>riment.

2. Here are some more words. Listen to the tape and repeat the words.

/ˈmaɪkrəʊfɪlm/	(microfilm)	/prɪˈzɜːv/	(preserve)
/ˈkjuːbɪkl/	(cubical)	/prezəˈveɪʃn/	(preservation)
/ˈkrɪstəlaɪz/	(crystallise)	/prɪˈzɜːvətɪv/	(preservative)
/ɪkˈspləʊʒn/	(explosion)	/ˈsekrətrɪ/	(secretary)
/ɪnˈspekt/	(inspect)	/sekrəˈteərɪəl/	(secretarial)
/prəˈpɔːʃn/	(proportion)	/ˈmɪstərɪ/	(mystery)
		/mɪˈstɪərɪəs/	(mysterious)

Notice that a change in stress often goes with a change in the pronunciation of some vowels as in *preserve* and *preservation*.

Now practise reading these words and phrases. Check your performance by listening to the tape. Pay special attention to the stresses and the weak forms in unstressed syllables. The words and phrases are printed in the key.

/tiː/
/ə ˈkʌp əv ˈtiː/
/hiː wɒnts ə ˈkʌp əv ˈtiː/

/θriː/
/ˈtʃæptə ˈθriː/
/ɪn ˈtʃæptə ˈθriː/

/ˈdaɪəɡræm/
/ðə ˈdaɪəɡræm/
/ðə ˈdaɪəɡræm ɪn ˈtʃæptə ˈθriː/

/wɜːdz/
/ˈfreɪzɪz/
/ˈwɜːdz ən ˈfreɪzɪz/
/ər ɒn ˈpeɪdʒ ˈten/
/ðə ˈwɜːdz ən ˈfreɪzɪz ər ɒn ˈpeɪdʒ ˈten/

3. Grammatical or structure words (such as articles, prepositions and pronouns) are usually unstressed. This can make it difficult for the learner to hear exactly what is being said. Some of your note-making tasks will give you practice in hearing these small but essential words (Decoding exercises). If you have problems here, this exercise will help you to identify them. Listen to the tape and write down what you hear. The answers are in the key.

1. . . . .

2. . . . .

3. . . . .

4. .... time

5. ....

6. ....

7. I saw ....

8. I saw ....

9. I saw ....

10. The chemical .... water.

11. The chemical .... water.

12. The chemical .... water.

13. The chemical .... water.

14. The chemicals .... water.

15. Not separately, ... same time.

16. ....

    this tank ....

    first solution ....

    .... second.

17. ....

    careful ....

    .... mixed up ....

    .... do ....

    .... explode.

18. ....

    last part ....,

    ....

    call the supervisor.

Word Building

In English, words are formed from other words in two ways:
a) By joining existing words, e.g. class + room = classroom. *Classroom* is a compound word; it is formed by compounding.
b) By adding syllables to the beginning or end of a word, e.g. in + effect + ive = ineffective. *Ineffective* is formed by derivation. *In-* and *-ive* are affixes. *In-* is called a prefix and *-ive* a suffix. Generally suffixes change the grammatical class of words (effect = n.; effective - adj.) but not the basic meaning. Prefixes, on the other hand, usually change the meaning.

Here are some common prefixes. Dictionaries usually list these and their meanings:

(*negation, not, opposite*)
non-	nonsense, non-toxic
dis-	displace, displease
mis-	mislead, misprint
im-	improbable, immobile
in-	insoluble, inoperative
il-	illegitimate, illogical
ir-	irreplaceable, irregular
un-	unbroken, unavoidable

(*one*)
mono- monochrome, monorail

(*two*)
bi- bicycle, bisect

(*three*)
tri- tricycle, triangle

(*again*)
re- relocate, rejoin

(*change* or *across*)
trans- transform, transport

(*out of* or *former*)
ex- extract, ex-president

Note Not all words beginning with these syllables include these meanings. Even so, if you become familiar with such prefixes — there are a number of others not noted above — you will have another resource for discovering the meanings of unfamiliar words.

Here are some common suffixes, listed according to their grammatical functions:

Nouns
-er, -or	researcher, supervisor
-ist	economist, geologist
-ance, -ence	endurance, permanence
-ment	displacement, government
-ness	hardness, brittleness
-ity	rarity, activity
-ion	connection, provision
-ing	building, meeting

Adjectives
-able, -ible   controllable, edible
-less   wingless, colourless
-ly, -y   lively, hardy
-ive   destructive, active
-ant, -ent   resistant, permanent
-ing   flying, hardening
-ed   hardened, purified

Verbs
-en   harden, darken
-fy, -ify   liquify, solidify
-ate   amalgamate, compensate
-ise, -ize   sterilise, randomize

4. From what you have read about word building in this unit, complete the following classification

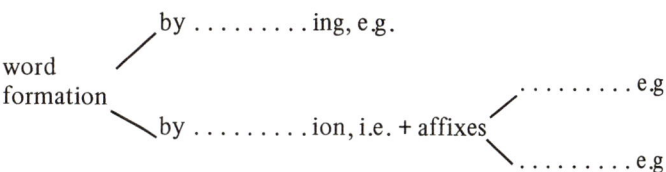

5. With the help of your dictionary, write down single words in the blank spaces below. Take care to note any changes in spelling.

a) To make beautiful.   = to ....

b) Someone who investigates.   = an ....

   This person's tasks and activities.   = his ....

c) The property of being flexible.   = its ....

d) He likes to destroy things.   = He's a .... person.

e) The slow-worm is a kind of lizard without legs.   = It is a .... lizard.

f) The heat will make the wax soft.   = It will .... it.

g) As the wax becomes soft, it changes colour.   = The .... wax changes colour.

h) When it is soft, the wax is brown.   = The .... wax is brown.

i) The fact that it is soft makes it suitable.   = Its .... makes it suitable.

5

6. With the help of your dictionary, write down the grammatical class of each of the words in the left-hand column and in the right-hand column write down the changed form indicated in the brackets.

   e.g. erupt   (v.)   eruption .... (noun)

   activity   (   )   .... (adjective)

   forceful   (   )   .... (verb)

   audible   (   )   .... (n.)

   aggression   (   )   .... (adj.)

   expand   (   )   .... (adj.)

   red   (   )   .... (v.)

   pressure   (   )   .... (v.)

   chemist   (   )   .... (n.)

7. Here is a specimen entry from a dictionary. Study it with the help of the notes below to see what kind of information it gives you. Notice changes of pronunciation and stress in derivatives.

> **dic·tate** /dɪkˈteɪt US: ˈdɪkteɪt/ vt, vi **1** [VP6A,2A,14] ∼ **(to)**, say or read aloud (words to be written down by another or others): to ∼ a letter to a secretary. The teacher ∼d a passage to the class. **2** [VP6A,14] ∼ **(to)**, state with the force of authority: to ∼ terms to a defeated enemy. **3** [VP3A] ∼ **to**, order: I won't be ∼d to, I refuse to accept orders from you. □ n /ˈdɪkteɪt/ (usu pl) direction or order (esp given by reason, conscience, etc): the ∼s of common sense. Follow the ∼s of your conscience. **dic·ta·tion** /dɪkˈteɪʃn/ n **1** [U] dictating; being dictated to: The pupils wrote at their teacher's ∼. **2** [C] passage, etc that is dictated.
> **dic·ta·tor** /dɪkˈteɪtə(r) US: ˈdɪkteɪtər/ n ruler who has absolute authority, esp one who has obtained such power by force or in an irregular way ∼**·ship** /-ʃɪp/ n [C,U] (country with) government by a ∼. **dic·ta·torial** /ˌdɪktəˈtɔːrɪəl/ adj of or like a ∼: ∼ial government; overbearing; fond of giving orders: his ∼ial manner. **dic·ta·tori·ally** /-əlɪ/ adv

a) The dot in the middle of the headword shows where you can break it up if you wish to write part of it on a new line.
b) US: In American English, the stress is on the first syllable.

c) vt, vi. It is a verb and can be used transitively or intransitively.
[VP6A, 2A, 14] This refers you to the list of verb patterns and shows that you can use this verb in one of three ways:
>> He dictated a letter. [6A]
>> He dictated. [2A]
>> He dictated a letter to his secretary. [14]
>> but not   *He dictated her a letter.
d) Three definitions are given. The second one follows the grammatical patterns 6A and 14. The third one follows a new pattern, 3A (i.e. verb + preposition + object): He tried to dictate to me.
e) □ This symbol shows a change of grammatical class. **Dictate** as a noun is stressed on the first syllable.
f) Notice that **dictation** can be either an uncountable (mass) or a countable (count) noun. The former use is much commoner and therefore is mentioned first.
Both: The next task is dictation. [U]
  and: I will return yesterday's dictations. [C]
are possible.

8. Study the entry for **dictator** to see what information is given.

Unit 2 Note-making

To study effectively you must be able to make effective notes. One of the aims of this course is to make you an effective note-maker. *You should study this unit frequently as you work through the book.*

Good notes require   speed
                              accuracy
                              clarity

Note-making is a two-stage process:

1. the notes are taken from
    a) a piece of writing
    b) what someone says
  or they are written as a plan of
    c) what you want to write
    d) what you are going to say;

2. the notes are read and used later.

There are three elements in good note-making.

what you do (activity)	**how you do it** (skill)
1. •reading/listening and planning	•accurate analysis of text and planning
2. •note-making	•rapid note writing
3. •note reading and development as writing or speaking	•accurate and easy read-back

Look at this example of how notes are taken from a short lecture (a spoken text), then used in the writing of a report.

Text

1 Our first experiment illustrating expansion through heat requires the apparatus before us: a ring on a metal stand, a metal ball and a Bunsen burner. Having lit the Bunsen, you see how easily the ball can be passed through the ring. It doesn't touch any part as it goes through. Now, I'm taking it out and
5 applying heat from the burner. I'll do that for several seconds . . . Well, let's see what happens when I try to pass the ball through the ring this time. The metal ball will not go through. Since the ring has remained untouched by the heat, we must conclude that the ball has increased in volume, that is to say, it has expanded.

Notes   **Expans. of Metal**

                Apparat.   a) ring on stand
                                            b) metal ball
                                            c) Bun. burn.

                Exper.   1. cold ball passed through ring
                                            2. ball heat. sev. secs.
                                            3. " wd. not go through
                                            4. ∴ vol. of ball ↑ – i.e. ball expand.

Lab report   **Expansion of Metal**

                Apparatus   The apparatus consisted of a ring on a stand, a metal ball chained to the top of the stand, and a Bunsen burner.

                Experiment   First, the metal ball was passed through the ring without touching any part of it. Then, heat from the Bunsen burner was applied to the ball for several seconds. When an attempt was then made to pass the heated ball through the ring, it was found that it would not go through.

                Conclusion   The heat had caused the volume of the metal ball to increase through expansion.

We have looked at the three basic skills of note-making. Here they are related to their sub-skills.

Skill   **Sub-skill**

accurate analysis
1. Identify the subject of the text. Establish what it is about, and devise a title for the notes.
2. Identify the main points of the text. When the text is written, mark the most important points by underlining, boxing, ringing, colouring over, or a combination of these.
3. Sort out the logic of the text. Establish which example relates to which point, etc.
4. Re-order the points made in the text, if necessary, according to its logic.

rapid note-making
5. Use abbreviations for speed.
6. Use symbols for speed and to show the logical relationships within the text.
7. Omit all unnecessary language for speed.
8. Use the space of the page to lay the notes out clearly.
9. Use numbers and letters to identify and distinguish different points, secondary points etc., examples etc.

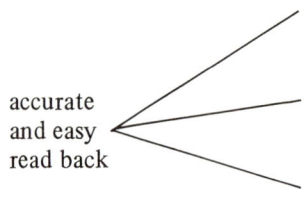

accurate and easy read back

10. The use of clear lay-out, numbers and letters assists fast and accurate interpretation of the notes.
11. Systematic use of abbreviations, symbols and omissions ensures rapid and accurate recall of the meaning of the notes.
12. Good notes represent the essential intermediate stage to good writing, effective speaking and successful problem-solving etc.

Abbreviations

Purpose

Abbreviations are used in order to make notes more quickly. Any word (except 'a'!) may be abbreviated. You must decide:
a) which words to abbreviate — obviously the most common in a text, or the language of your study, or of English in general.
b) how to abbreviate them — you should use the shortest abbreviation which will be meaningful when you read back. An abbreviation is useless if you do not understand it immediately when you are reading your notes.

Types

There are four main types of abbreviation in general use.

Type A: abbreviations of English or Latin phrases, in which the first letters, or sometimes syllables, of the words are given, as in p.a. (the abbreviation of the Latin phrase *per annum*) meaning *yearly*.

Type B: abbreviations of one-syllable words, consisting of the first letter only, as in b. meaning *born*, or the first and last letters of the word, as in yr meaning *year*.

Type C: abbreviations of polysyllabic (more than one syllable) words, in which the first letters of certain syllables are used, as in cg meaning *centigramme*, or the first and last letters of certain syllables, as in bldg meaning *building*.
This type of abbreviation is often used with the vocabulary of science.

Type D (the most common): abbreviations of polysyllabic words, consisting of the shortest possible abbreviations which are easily recognisable, as in doz. meaning *dozen*, geog. meaning *geography* and geol. meaning *geology*.

Full stops

Note the following general rules:
1. A full stop after an abbreviation indicates that a word has been cut short before the end, as in Prof. meaning *Professor*. If an abbreviation contains the final letter of a word, it is not usually followed by a full stop, as in yr meaning *year*.
2. Scientific measurements, such as km, mm, kg, are usually written without full stops.
3. Common abbreviations of English phrases are often written without full stops, as in amu meaning *atomic mass unit*, whereas phrases consisting of foreign words are usually abbreviated with full stops, as in i.e. and op. cit. (Latin).

10

Selected standard abbreviations

The following lists of standard abbreviations are drawn from the English of general study (ch., ed., e.g.) and from specific subject areas (CNS, colloq., kWh).
Do not try to memorise all of them but select those which you think will be of most use to you.

Type A

A.D. (Latin)	years after the birth of Christ
A.H. (Lat.)	years after the Hegira
amu	atomic mass unit
c. (Lat.)	about, approximately
°C	degrees Celsius/Centigrade
cc	cubic centimetre(s)
CNS	central nervous system
e.g. (Lat.)	for example
etc. (Lat.)	*et cetera*, and so on
°F	degrees Fahrenheit
i.e. (Lat.)	that is
NB (Lat.)	take note that
op. cit. (Lat.)	in the book mentioned previously
p.a. (Lat.)	in one year
s.g.	specific gravity

Type B

b.	born		nr	near
d.	died		p.	page
E	East		pp.	pages
g	gramme		pt	part
hr	hour		rd	road
ht	height		S	South
Hz	herts (cycles per second)		vb	verb
J	joule (unit of energy, work and heat)		W	West
			wk	week
Mt	Mount		wt	weight
N	North		yr	year
n.	noun			

Type C

bldg	building		km	kilometre(s)
cf (Lat.)	compare		kW	kilowatt(s)
cg	centigramme(s)		kWh	kilowatt-hour(s)
cl	centilitre(s)		mb	millibar(s)
cm	centimetre(s)		mm	millimetre(s)
kg	kilogramme(s)		no. (Lat.)	number

Type D

Note that although an abbreviation usually refers to the noun form, it may also refer to the adjective, adverb and verb forms.

adj.	adjective
adv.	adverb
alg.	algebra
anat.	anatomy
anon.	anonymous
amp(s)	ampere(s)
approx.	approximate(ly)
arch.	architecture
archaeol.	archaeology
arith.	arithmetic
astron.	astronomy
bet.	between
biog.	biography
biol.	biology
bot.	botany
C, cent.	century
ch.	chapter
colloq.	colloquial
cont.	continued
def.	definition
deg.	degrees
diam.	diameter
diff.	difference
doz.	dozen
ed.	edition, edited by
esp.	especially
fig.	figure
fut.	future
geog.	geography
geol.	geology
geom.	geometry
hist.	history
in.(ins)	inch(es)
indiv.	individual
indust.	industry
intro.	introduction
lang.	language
lat.	latitude
lect.	lecture
log.	logarithm
long.	longitude
maths	mathematics
med.	medicine
max.	maximum
min.	minimum
mod.	modern
neg.	negative
partic.	particular
pop.	1. population 2. popular

Prof.	Professor
prep.	1. preparatory
	2. preposition
ref.	reference
rev.(s)	revolution(s)
sol.	solution
sub.	subject
trig.	trigonometry
Univ.	University
v.	very
vel.	velocity

Further abbreviations The following abbreviations are used in the note-making exercises and not included in the previous lists. Remember that you can also devise your own abbreviations.

abs.	1. absent
	2. absorption
acc.	according to
act.	1. actual
	2. activity, action
apert.	aperture
b + w	black and white
breath.	breathing
chann.	channel
cd	could
coll.	collection
conserv.	conservative
construct.	constructive
cont.	1. continue
	2. continent
convect.	convection
cov.	cover
destruct.	destructive
diag.	diagonal
div.	divide
empt.	empty
evt	event
exp.	experience
ext.	external
extract.	extraction
gdn	garden
info.	information
inhib.	inhibit
int.	1. internal
	2. interior
interp.	interpretation
lngth	length
lev.(s)	level(s)
move.	movement
musc.	muscle
phys.	physical

pl.	plate
pred.	predict
prob.	problem
pt	point
reg.	regular
rm	room
sev.	several
shd	should
simul.	simultaneously, at the same time
soc.	society, social
sol.	solution
stim.	stimulus
temp.	1. temperature 2. temporary
tens.	tension
trop.	tropic
typ.	typical
usu.	usual(ly)
wd	would

Symbols

Purpose

Symbols are used in note making:
a) for speed
b) to show the relationships between words and within the text.
   e.g. a sentence such as this:
   The earth's circuit round the sun takes just over 365 days.
   may be noted like this: Earth's circ. rd sun => 365 dys

Types

Most symbols are taken from mathematics. Some of the most useful are given in the list below. Note the variety of meanings that one symbol can convey, and that those expressing a verb or verb phrase do not show tense.

+	and, plus
−	less, minus
=	is, equals, consists of, is the same as, there is
≠	is not, does not equal, does not consist of, is different from
≡	is equivalent to
>	is greater than, is more than, is over
<	is less than
→	gives, produces, leads to, provides, results in, is re-written as
←	is given by, is produced by, results from, comes from
↗	rises, increases by, grows to/by
↘	falls, decreases by, declines
∴	therefore, so
∵	because, as, since
@	at
:	indicates example(s) following
( )	used around explanation of a point
°	degrees
′	minutes, feet
″	inches *or* ditto marks − i.e. repeat the word above
BUT	but, however, although

Practice

Read this short passage:

> Musical instruments can be divided into two basic groups: those which are played with the hands alone, and those for which both hands and mouth are needed. The former group includes the keyboard, stringed and percussion instruments, and the latter the brass and woodwind.

Now think about the passage. Decide what its subject is, and what title to give the notes. Decide which parts should be omitted, which should be changed, which may be abbreviated, and which can be expressed by symbols.

Look at the analysed passage. The markings show how the text is to be translated into note form. The markings conform to the system below:

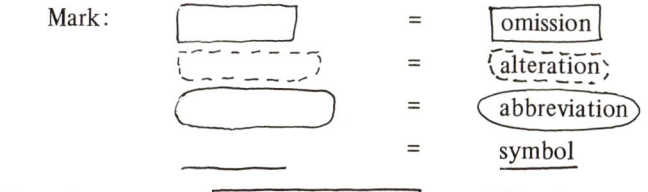

Musical instruments can be divided into two basic groups; those which are played with the hands alone, and those for which both hands and mouth are needed. The former group includes the keyboard, stringed and percussion instruments, and the latter the brass and woodwind.

Finally, refer to the analysis and see how it has been translated into note form below, with the space of the page used for a clear lay-out, numbers and letters to identify major and minor points, examples etc.,

Music. Insts
2 bas. gps.
a) play. hands only e.g. keybd, string, percuss.
b) "   "   + mouth e.g. brass & woodwd

Analyse the short passage below in the way described above, then make notes on each one.

1. Another concept basic to linguistics is that of paradigmatic relationships within the language. Take the sentence, so popular with linguists:

    The cat sat on the mat.

    The cat could be replaced by The dog, or John, or even, The elephant, and the sentence would remain perfectly grammatical. Cat, dog, elephant and John, therefore, are said to have a paradigmatic relationship. Obviously, they make up a set, and a set which would exclude such words as sat and on.

2. Children born prematurely have a decreased chance of survival due to their general weakness and low weight — sometimes less than a kilo. An incubator greatly improves the chances of survival of the premature infant. This machine provides the most ideal environment for the individual requirements of the child. The variable factors of most importance are that the surroundings are sterile, that is, germ-free, and that the temperature can be made as high as 37°C. Of equal importance are the oxygen concentration and the high relative humidity which it is possible to obtain.

3. The air in the gap between the walls of the flask is removed, thus creating a vacuum. The walls themselves are silvered so as to minimise heat loss due to radiation. In this way, the interior of the flask is insulated, and contents placed in it will remain hot or cold for several hours.

4. We have tangible evidence of what the inhabitants of Pompeii were like, thanks to the ingenuity of the Italian archaeologist Giuseppe Fiorelli more than a century ago. On the day of the eruption, the unluckier citizens were overwhelmed by falling rock, lava and ash from Vesuvius. In time the ash, which had buried the bodies feet-deep, hardened, and the corpses decomposed inside their envelopes of volcanic residue. Fiorelli discovered that by breaking a small hole into the spaces which had surrounded the bodies, and then forcing liquid plaster in, a cast could be made. The plaster casts so formed showed, when set, the physical appearance and clothing of the victims of this 1st century A.D. catastrophe in amazing detail.

Unit 3   Earthquakes

Reading

Pre-read
1. Have you ever experienced an earthquake or seen an active volcano?
2. Do you know why such events occur?
3. Is the earth really just a very large ball of hard rock?
4. If you drilled a hole in the ground and went on drilling deeper and deeper, what would you find?

Text

Para 1
1 The planet earth seems to us a very stable and unmoving place — continents of solid rock surrounded by the oceans. In one sense, of course, it is stable, or our kind of life would be impossible. But when we experience or hear about violent natural events like earthquakes and volcanoes, we also get some idea
5 of the great forces at work under its surface.

P2
1 In fact the earth is a very complex object, made up of many layers. What we are familiar with is only the upper surface of the 'skin', or crust. This crust is altogether rather more than 100 km deep. The outer crust, of a depth of approximately 8 km, is made mostly of very hard rock, a kind of granite.
5 This makes up the continents or major land masses. Below it is a much thicker layer, the inner crust, also made of a hard but different kind of rock, basalt. Beneath this lies the upper mantle, a semi-fluid layer about 600 km deep, where temperatures reach 1,500°C. The lower mantle is more rigid, because of the great pressures at those depths. It extends a further 2,900 km
10 towards the centre of the earth and has a temperature twice that of the layer immediately above it.

P3
1 Within the mantle is the core. This again is divided into two layers, the outer and the inner. The former consists of molten nickel and iron and has a temperature of 3,900°C. The latter, of the same constituents, is, however, relatively solid, again because of the great pressure at those depths. The
5 temperature of the inner core is about 900°C higher than that of the outer core and its diameter is approximately 4,300 km.

1. Content skim
1. What is the topic of this passage?
2. What does it list in detail?
3. How many of these does it mention?

2. Comprehension scan

P1.2   What does 'it' refer to?
P1.5   What does 'its' refer to?
P2.5   What does 'This' refer to?
P2.5   What does 'it' refer to?
       What other layer is made of hard rock?
P2.7   What does 'this' refer to?
P2.8   'more rigid' than what?
P2.9   What depths are referred to as 'those depths'?
P2.9   What does 'It' refer to?
P2.10 What is 'the layer immediately above it'?
P3.2   What does 'the former' refer to?
P3.3   What does 'the latter' refer to?
P3.4   Why is 'again' used here?
P3.6   What does 'its' refer to?

17

| 3. Identifying and describing | Label the diagram and complete the table below it. |

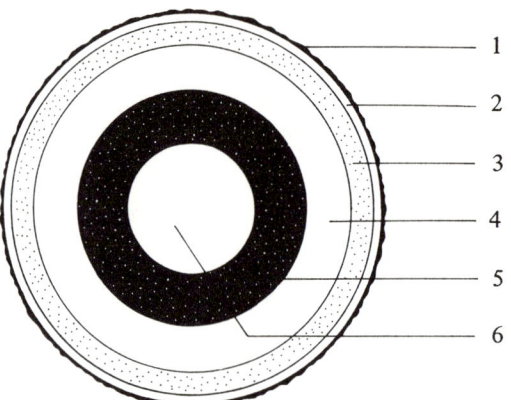

	Constituents/ Consistency	Temperature	Depth
1			
2			
3			
4			
5			
6			

Listening

4. Decoding

As you listen to Part 1 of the talk, complete the following:

An earthquake is a shaking movement or tremor ....

.... surface ....

.... Some ....

.... that we need sensitive instruments

.... them

while the most severe ....

.... terrible destruction. Most ....,

especially large ones, are ....
a fracture or splitting of the earth's crust. This happens when the stress .....
.... rocks
becomes greater than their strength. These ....
.... originate in the mantle or are ....
.... slow movements in the continental plates, the thick parts ....
.... crust. Earthquakes ....
.... in association with volcanoes and some
are caused by drilling ....
.... deep in the ground.

5. Controlled note-making

As you listen to Part 2, complete the following notes. Each space is for one word, abbreviation or symbol. In this unit and the next one, full words are given in brackets after abbreviations to help you.

1. Es orig. (Earthquakes originate) in .... or ....

    Latter ← move. (movement) .... in

    semi- .... mantle.

2. .... of focus found by .... timing of

    ....

    Kinds of wave: a) ....

    　　　　　　　　b) ....

    　　　　　　　a) = i) ....

    　　　　　　　　　 ii) ....

    ii) travel at c. .... i)

3. Meas. (Measurement) of ....

    .... bet. (between) i) & ii) → est. (estimate) of

    .... of ....

19

6. Guided note-making

As you listen to Part 3, complete the following notes:

Measurement of earthquakes

Instrument:

Scales 1

      2

Stnd of meas. (Standard of measurement) of 2:

Pt (Point) 4:

" 5:

" 6:

" 8:

" 10:

" 12:

7. Classifying

The following are extracts from reports of earthquakes. Decide in each case what point the earthquake probably measured on the scale you have heard about. If the evidence does not enable you to identify it exactly as one of the points described, mark it with an X or indicate the two closest points.

1. Reports are coming in of an earthquake in China. The epicentre is located near the town of Tanshang, which has only recently been rebuilt after a severe earthquake in 1976. The extent of the damage is so far not clear but some casualties have occurred, mainly as a result of falling masonry from roofs and balconies.

   . . . .

2. The President has declared a state of emergency to deal with the consequences of the earthquake which hit the area around Lake Van last night. Casualties are said to be very high and in some villages, where older and less substantial buildings predominate, it is said that not a house remains standing.

   . . . .

3. North Lancashire received the brunt of the earthquake, though it was felt as far south as parts of Cheshire. One resident of Carnforth, Dr D. Tye, has this to say: 'I was just reaching for a bottle to refill my glass when there was this extraordinary feeling that the house was moving under me. The bottle almost fell over, but fortunately I caught it in time. The lampshade started to sway and there were some very odd noises, but luckily everything seems to be intact.'

   . . . .

4. Only one death has been reported, the result of a falling chimney which brought down with it the ceiling of the bedroom immediately below. The weight of falling masonry caused the bedroom floor to give way and Mr Wheeler, who was in the sitting-room, was buried under several tons of rubble.

. . . .

5. 'I was driving along the coast road when the car suddenly lurched to one side. At first I thought a tyre had gone but then I saw telegraph poles collapsing like matchsticks and the road looked as if it had turned to liquid, moving about and cracking, like some sort of syrup with a crust on top. It was then that the rocks came down across the road and I had to leave the car. When I got back to town across the hill, well, as I said, there wasn't much left.'

. . . .

6. 'There was a sharp sound like something cracking and I realised I could see daylight through the wall; then just as quickly the gap closed again and all you can see now is this line running up from the door. They say it won't be a big job to patch it up. My neighbour wasn't so lucky. His wall cracked but it didn't close up again, so now he has an extra view across the valley.'

. . . .

Unit 4   Energy Sources

Reading

Pre-read

1. Is your home heated in winter and, if so, how? How is your food cooked?
2. Which kinds of fuel are used in your country to make electricity for industry and the home?
3. Are there any problems or difficulties in getting enough energy or paying for it?
4. Do you think the situation will have changed much in a hundred years' time and, if so, why?

Text

Para 1   1   In technologically advanced societies, the enormous consumption of energy per head is one aspect of the ever-increasing pressure man is placing on his environment. Early industrial man used three times as much energy as his agricultural ancestor; modern man is using three times as much as his
5   industrial ancestor. If present trends continue, the rate of consumption will have tripled again by the end of the century. The problem lies in the fact that most of our current energy sources are finite. The hard truth is that a day will come when there is little or no exploitable coal, oil or natural gas anywhere. The sharp rise in the price of oil over the last decade has been
10   unpleasant for many parts of the world but in the long run it is beneficial, partly because it discourages waste and partly because it has forced many nations to seek ways of developing better and more permanent sources of energy.

P2   1   Energy sources may initially be divided into two kinds: non-renewable (i.e. finite) and renewable. The former group includes coal, oil, gas and, in the long run, nuclear; the latter hydropower, solar power and wind power. The energy from all these sources ultimately derives from the sun. There is
5   a further source — geothermal — which depends on the earth's own heat. In practice this may be classed as non-renewable as it is exploitable in only a few places and even there is limited.

P3   1   There is a second distinction that is often made, that between conventional and non-conventional energy sources. A conventional energy source is one which is at present widely exploited. In view of the points made in para. 1 (above) it will be realised that, broadly, the conventional sources are the
5   non-renewable ones. This is not entirely true, however, as a good deal of oil is locked up in solid form in rock (tar sands and oil shale) and this source, though non-renewable, is also non-conventional, since it has not so far been developed very much. In what follows, the earlier distinction, rather than this one, will be assumed when comparing different energy sources.

P4   1   Energy sources may be compared from several points of view. You will hear about some of these in the talk, but first it is important to explain the terms used:
   a) Renewability. This has been referred to.
5   b) Availability. Some energy sources may be excellent from some points of view but unlikely to contribute much at any time because of their limited geographical availability.
   c) Cost and efficiency. Some sources may be cheap but highly inefficient, even to a point where they are not practicable. Coal, for instance, though

10 certainly practicable and comparatively cheap, is not very efficient (the efficiency even of a modern power station is only 35%). Geothermal sources, though in a sense free, would, in order to be maintained, end up by using more energy than they produced. Others, like oil, may be comparatively efficient but are in danger of becoming prohibitively expensive.

1. Content skim

1. Look at the title of the unit and the first sentence of each paragraph. What is the topic of the passage?
2. How does it deal with this topic?
3. What is the main division between different kinds?
4. How many ways of comparing sources are given?

2. Comprehension scan

P1.5 What are these 'trends'?
P1.6 What is 'the problem'?
P1.11 What 'discourages waste'?
P1.12 'Better and more permanent' than what?
P2.3 What does 'the latter' refer to?
P2.4 Which sources are included in 'all'?
P2.7 Which word(s) could you add between 'there' and 'is limited'?
P3.1 What was the first distinction?
P3.3 What were 'the points' made in the first paragraph?
P3.6 What does 'this' refer to?
P3.8 What is the earlier distinction and what is this one?

3. Classifying and comparing

Using the grid below, list vertically in the left-hand column all sources of energy mentioned in the text. Then, from information given so far, place a tick in the appropriate box if an energy source has the feature noted at the head of the column. Mark with a cross if it does not. If the information is not provided, leave the box empty.

	renewable	available	low cost	efficient	non-polluting	not adding to earth's load
a) rivers						
b) seas						

Listening

4. Decoding

As you listen to Part 1, complete the following:

All forms of non-renewable energy sources are to a greater .... polluting, though the type of .... varies. Coal, in common with other fossil ...., produces sulphur dioxide, though in this respect gas compares very favourably with .... The combustion of fossil fuels also produces carbon dioxide in far greater quantities than plant life .... This carbon dioxide, by accumulating in ...., may well lead to global rises in temperature (called the 'greenhouse effect') .... could in time have a disastrous effect on climate. Nuclear fuel does not emit gases into the atmosphere when used, ... its own highly toxic waste products. Being solid , ... to control than the gases emitted by .... but their presence in growing quantities is potentially very dangerous indeed. All .... so far mentioned add to the earth's heat load and .... provide a long-term danger to the environment. The wide availability of fossil fuels, on the other hand, and the increasing availability of nuclear sources inevitably ensure that they will go on .... exploited for as long as they ....

5. Controlled note-making

As you listen to Part 2, complete the following notes, each space is for one word, abbreviation or symbol.

Tot. (Total) reserves .... ≡ ....
.... solar energy.
∴   a) .... for all
but   b) low .... → .... to use (cost, ...
         and cont. (continuous) ....)
but   c) Pos. (Possible) .... SE (solar energy) v. (very) ....

                    Advants (Advantages)   i) .... — ....
                                          ii) .... — ....
                                          iii) not + ...

6. Guided note-making   As you listen to Part 3, complete the following notes:

Hydropower

1. Nat. (Natural)
2. Damming rivers
        2 v. limited → serious effects:
            a) loss of
            b) silting of
            c)
3. Seas =
        a) greater avail. (availability)
    but b) not praticable
        c) "   "

∴ HP = SP (hydropower = solar power):equip. (equipment)
  Advants of 1, 2 & 3: a)
        b) not +

7. Classifying and comparing   From your notes, complete as far as possible the grid at 3, above.

8. Identifying   The following passage deals with three energy sources. Decide on the identity of A, B & C.

Source A, though comparatively cheap and widely available, will certainly disappear at some time. This will have certain advantages, however, in terms of the threat it poses — and has posed for a long time — to the environment. Source B is certainly becoming increasingly available, though it too will eventually run out. The dangers it poses to the environment are different but possibly greater. Source C is not a problem in this respect but it may not be convenient for other reasons to exploit it fully. The amount of space needed to develop it and its varying availability in any particular location are real disadvantages. On the other hand, one obvious advantage over the other sources is, of course, that it will never run out.

9. Writing   Write a short paragraph comparing three other sources about which you have information. Name the sources (i.e. do not use the code 'source A' etc). Use the previous paragraph to help you but do not try to follow it exactly.

Unit 5   The Whale

Reading

Pre-read

1. Does your country border on a sea or ocean where whales can be found?
2. What do whales look like and which group of living things do they belong to?
3. Are whales killed because, like many sharks, they are dangerous? Do people get eaten by whales?
4. Have you ever used or eaten anything that comes from the whale?
5. What difference would it make if all the whales disappeared or if men stopped catching them?

Text

Para 1
1 Whales are sea-living mammals*. They therefore breathe air but cannot survive on land. Some species are very large indeed and the blue whale, which can exceed 30 m in length, is the largest animal to have lived on earth. Superficially, the whale looks rather like a fish, but there are important differences
5 in its external structure: its tail consists of a pair of broad, flat, horizontal paddles (the tail of a fish is vertical) and it has a single nostril on the top of its large, broad head. The skin is smooth and shiny and beneath it lies a layer of fat (the blubber). This is up to 30 cm in thickness and serves to conserve heat and body fluids.

P2
1 There are two main groups of whale — toothed and toothless. The former includes the dolphin, the porpoise and the killer and sperm whales; the latter the grey, humpback, right and blue whales. Some toothed species, like the killer, feed on other large mammals such as the porpoise, while others — e.g.
5 the sperm whale — eat smaller forms of marine life. The mouth of the toothless whale is adapted to form a kind of sieve in which tiny marine animals are caught by a filtering process.

P3
1 Most whales move about in schools. While swimming they take in air and dive vertically, sometimes to great depths. Large whales can stay under water for up to 20 minutes. They then surface and expel air from their lungs, making the characteristic spout, which is audible from some distance and can be seen
5 largely because of the concentration of condensing water vapour in the expelled gases.

P4
1 Different species of whale are distributed widely throughout the world, from the North Atlantic to the Antarctic, and they have been hunted by man for many centuries. The oil has been much prized for use in cosmetics, the manufacture of margarine, as a lubricant for delicate mechanisms and in the soften-
5 ing of leather. The meat is used for both human and animal consumption. Indeed, in Japan it has been a staple protein source for many centuries. Whale bone, in processed form, has commercial uses but its use as such to strengthen corsets has disappeared along with corsets as fashions have changed. There is one other curious product of the whale, ambergris. This is a wax-like secre-
10 tion of the intestine, produced to deal with irritants, such as bones, which a toothed whale may swallow. It is sometimes found floating on the sea or

*Def. Mammals are air-breathing, warm-blooded animals which nourish their young with milk. With one or two exceptions — not including the whale — the young are born live rather than in egg form.

lying on beaches in greyish or blackish lumps. It is used, in tiny quantities, in the manufacture of perfume, where it serves to fix and enhance the various scents employed.

P5 1 The commercial value of the whale has led to drastic depletions of whale stocks and pressures of many kinds are making it very hard to achieve adequate protection for certain species. In the talk, you will hear something of the history of whaling and of the present critical situation of this mag-
5 nificent animal.

1. Content skim

1. What, in general, is the passage about?
2. Read the first sentence of each paragraph and decide on the probable topic of each.

2. Vocabulary development

a) Write down up to five words from the text to do with whales. Look these up in your dictionary; note the pronunciation beside each and write a brief note about the meaning.
b) Write down up to five other words from the text which you think might be more generally useful. Note down how each word is used in the passage and then compare this with information given in your dictionary.

3. Guided note-making

When you are satisfied that you understand the passage, complete the following notes:

Whales

1. Family:

2. Visible characts:

   a)

   b)

   c)

   d)

3. Main divs:

   a)   e.g.

   b)   e.g.

4. Food:

   a)

   b)

5. Behav.:

6. Distrib.:

27

7. Parts used by man:

   a)

   b)

   c)

   d)

Listening

4. Decoding

As you listen to Part 1 of the talk, complete the following:

The earliest people to engage in .... in an organised way were the Basques, who began to exploit the right .... north Atlantic in the 12th and 13th .... They would go from the shore .... , harpoon .... and return with their catch .... This kind of whaling spread to northern grounds, where .... by the Dutch, English and Norwegians. In the 18th and 19th centuries, the United States of America .... whaling nation, working in the Indian Ocean and the Pacific. Their bases were large ocean-going vessels which could .... for up to five .... and the whales, caught from ...., were cut up on deck .... stored below. During the same period, whaling stations .... in the Antarctic harbours from which boats ...., make their ...., so that the whales could be processed ....

5. Controlled note-making As you listen to Part 2, complete the following notes; each space is for one word, abbreviation or symbol.

1. 19thC develops: .... and ....
   .... gun. → catch .... Ws, e.g. the
   ....

2. 20thC .... : .... ships. Can ....
   & .... p ....
   + use of .... & ....

3. Results: Depletion of ....
   e.g. 1930s ....
   1968   "   "   ....

4. Dangers: Destruct. of ....
   "   "   ....

6. Guided note-making As you listen to Part 3, complete the following notes:

1. Organis.:

2. Yr:

3. Purp.:

4. 1980 props made:

   a)

   b)

   c)

   d)

5. Prop(s) accepted:

6. Fut.:

7. Identifying Decide in each of the following extracts whether the species in question *could* be a whale. If you think so, mark the extract with an X. If not, underline the feature or features which show that it could not be.
1. The skin, which is hard and scaly, is greyish in colour, thus helping to camouflage it from predators when underwater. It tends to feed in the shallows and is rarely found more than 100 m from land.
2. It feeds on squid and some species of fish which are to be found at moderate depths. The young are weaned at a few months, though they do not become fully independent until some time after that.
3. Forward movement is effected by moving the tail swiftly from side to side so that its flat surface pushes against the water. All members of this group are surface feeders, depending on minute forms of marine life which are strained through the mouth.

29

4. Although naturally timid, they are capable of friendship with man. If you are patient, one may soon poke out its nose to sniff the offered food and, from these small beginnings, it is possible to train some specimens to respond to different kinds of signal and perform tricks, which they seem to enjoy as much as the onlookers.
5. They have been hunted by man for centuries and, in places, provide a main source of food, but it is probably for the fine leather obtained from the skin that they have been most prized.
6. Fishermen cast nets in the area in order to catch the fish below them. In the process of drawing in the nets, a good many get caught under water and, on being hauled into the boats with the fish, are found to have died from drowning.

8. Writing

Using your notes to Part 3 of the talk, write a brief paragraph on the organisation you heard about.

Unit 6   Silicon Chips

Reading

Pre-read
1. Do radios look different now compared with 25 years ago? If so, can you think of any reasons for this?
2. Why were there no pocket calculators or digital watches 25 years ago?
3. Why are wires for conducting electricity covered in plastic?
4. If you dropped a piece of clothing onto an electric fire and it started to burn, how would you put it out?
5. How do you control electricity in the home?
6. Why is it often important to notice the colour of the wires when you attach a plug to a piece of electrical equipment?

Text

Para 1 1 Until the 1950s items of electrical equipment like radios had to be fairly large, mainly because they contained a number of valves — glass tubes built into the electrical circuit, looking a little like electric light bulbs. Inside the tube was a vacuum — or sometimes a gas — through which electrons could
5 pass. These components were really like switches — they controlled the direction and strength of the current passing through them. They had to warm up before they worked properly; they took up a lot of space; they eventually burned out and had to be replaced; also they were fragile, so dropping or knocking a radio often meant expensive repairs. Early computers had valves
10 but they were in consequence slow in operation and very limited in complexity because of the problems of size and maintenance.

P2 1 In 1947 the first transistors were produced at the Bell Telephone Laboratories in the USA. The transistor does not incorporate a vacuum or gas-filled tube, but the electricity passes through solid material. It is for this reason that transistors mark the beginning of what is known as solid-state technology.

P3 1 In the late fifties technologists developed a way of printing circuits onto sheets of material. In this way, the size of electrical equipment began to decrease even further: instead of separate valves mounted on a large framework and connected by wires, both the transistors and their connections were combined in single, small, tough units.

P4 1 The use of silicon is basic to the developments which have taken place since the fifties. This element has special electrical properties. It is a semiconductor, half way between a full conductor such as copper and an insulator like plastic. By adding small amounts of other chemicals to pieces of silicon
5 and then joining the resulting different types together in various ways, very fast, efficient 'switches' can be produced.

P5 1 As manufacturing processes grew more and more sophisticated it became possible to pack more and more individual transistors onto a single piece of silicon (called a chip). These chips are at most 1 cm square and about ½ mm thick. In 1960 a chip could hold 1 transistor. Today it can contain as many as
5 a million.

P6 1 Silicon chips are changing our world at an enormous pace: they affect or will affect all aspects of our lives — industry, transportation, finance, education, medicine, communication, domestic and recreational spheres. By using microtechnology, computers can now be made with an almost infinite operational
5 capacity. The cost is actually decreasing; their speed of operation is increasing;

31

P7 1 In the talk that follows you will hear how silicon chips are manufactured. Remember that the simplest transistor consists of two kinds of silicon in close contact, the difference depending on which impurity is added to each part. The first stage of the process consists in the production of a single crystal of
 5 very pure silicon. The crystal is in the shape of a long bar of about 10 cm in diameter and any chemical impurity which is needed to make one component of the transistors is added to the silicon while it is still liquid. The solidified bar is then cut into circular pieces about ½ mm thick. These are known as wafers and each one when cut up will yield perhaps a hundred chips.

1. Content skim

1. Read the first sentence of each paragraph and decide what the passage in general is about.
2. What particular development does the passage lead up to?
3. What is the topic of each paragraph?

2. Comprehension scan

P1.5 Which 'components' are referred to?
P1.7 What does 'they' refer to?
P2.2 What does incorporate such a tube?
P2.3 'Solid material' rather than what?
P2.3 What is the reason referred to?
P3.4 Which development(s) made this possible?
P4.2 Which element is referred to as 'this element'?
P4.5 Different types of what?
P4.6 Why is 'switches' in inverted commas?
P7.2 Where has this information already been given?

3. Note-making

List five limitations of valve systems. Beside each write any contrasting advantages of solid-state systems mentioned in the text.

1.

2.

3.

4.

5.

4. Identifying

Using information in the final paragraph, label diagrams 1–4. These show the first stages in the production of a silicon chip.

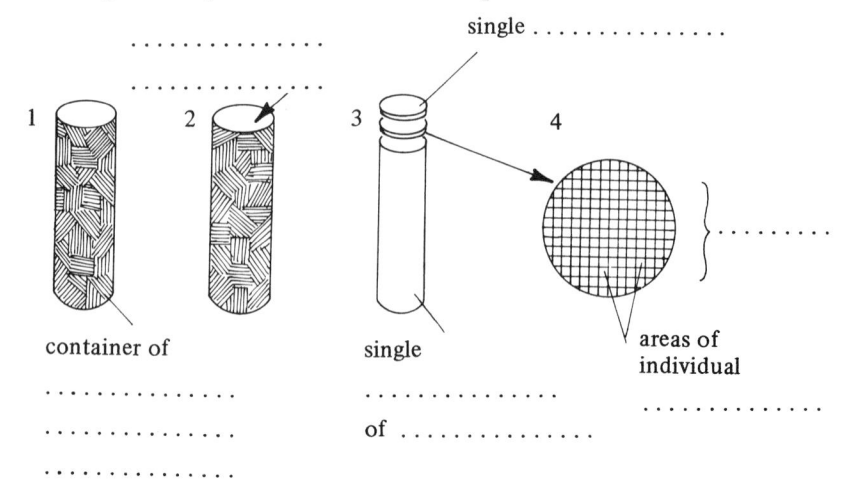

single . . . .

1   2   3   4

container of

single

areas of individual

of . . . .

Listening

In the talk the diagrams on pp. 32–6 are referred to. Look at them briefly first, but concentrate on making notes while you are listening to the talk. Later, you will be asked to complete these diagrams.

5. Decoding

As you listen to Part 1, complete the text below.

Now, each wafer is polished on one side until the .... extremely .... This is .... on which the circuits of .... will be built up. The .... are then baked in a very hot tubular furnace, as you can see in diagram 5. Right. This produces .... silicon oxide on .... of each .... Silicon .... will not conduct electricity, so the surface of each wafer is now an ...., while the silicon on the .... remains a .... A special photographic film called a photo-mask is now made. Diagram 6 shows a cross-section of this. This .... size as the wafer and has printed on it one layer of the correct micro-circuit. One .... will be made from the wafer. Parts of the .... will allow ultra-violet light to pass through and others .... The wafer is then coated with a, a chemical substance called photo-resist which becomes hard when .... light falls on it. Now, if you look at diagram 7, there, see that. The photo-mask is placed over the wafer .... exposed to ultra-violet light. The photo-resist not .... to UV light remains soft and this is then washed off with acid, as you can see in diagrams .... Next the layer of

33

silicon oxide underneath the ....
.... photo-resist is washed off and finally the hard .....
.... is
removed. The ....
.... of each chip on the wafer now shows the pattern of the ....
.... where the
silicon ....,
surrounded by the remaining ....
.... Now for these steps, you want to look at diagrams
....

6. Controlled note-making

As you listen to Part 2, complete these notes. Each space is for one word, abbreviation or symbol.

1. Objective: Add. of ....
.... to certain .... silicon.

Method:
   a)   .... placed in ...., cont.
               .... chemical in form of ....
               (chem. not .... silicon ....)
   b)   Chem. enters ....
      → Each chip 2 .... of .... + partial
           .... of ....

2. Objective: Add. of .... connections.
Method:
      Wafer .... to .... of ....
      (us. ....).
      → 1 complete .... of
           .... + ...

7. Guided note-making

As you listen to Part 3, complete the following notes:

Final Steps in Process

1. Each chip

    Rejects:

2. Wafers

3. Each chip

4. Wires

5. Incorporated

8. Identifying Label these diagrams. They show the remaining stages in the production of a silicon chip.

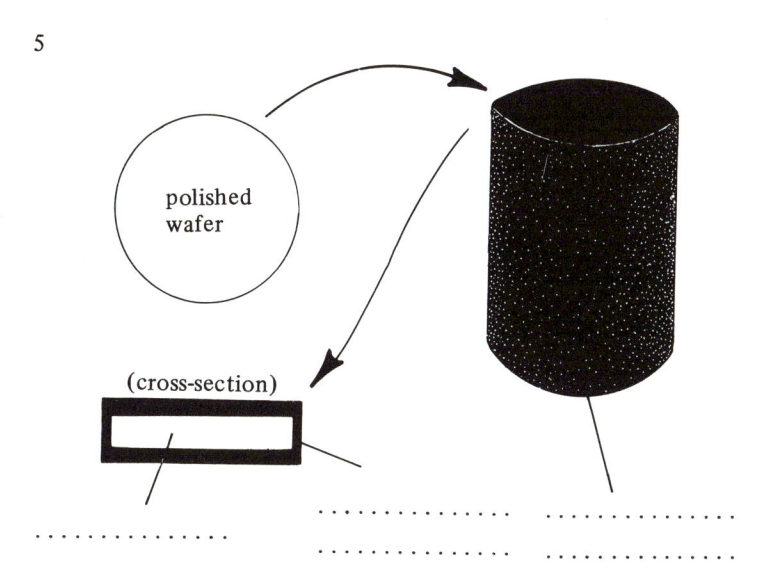

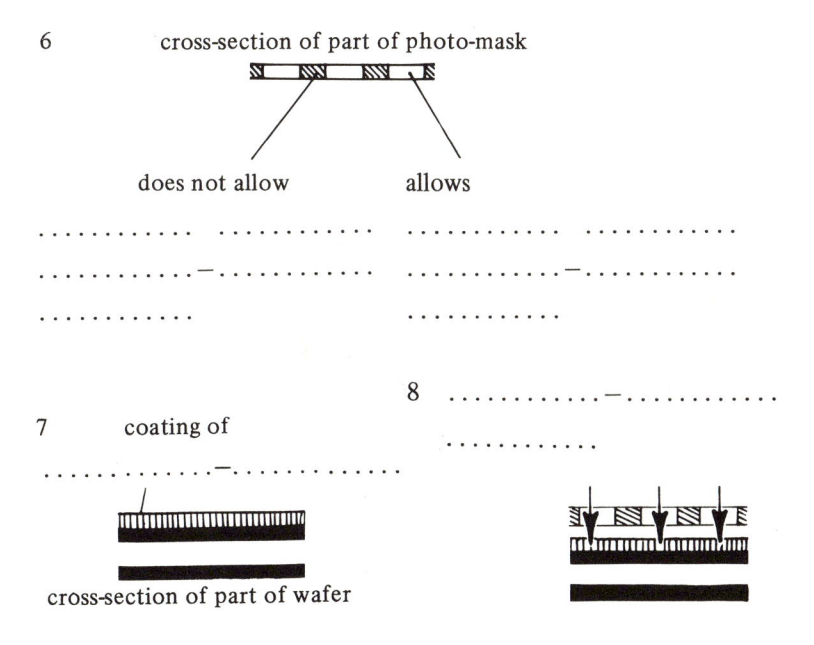

5

polished wafer

(cross-section)

....
                 ....

6   cross-section of part of photo-mask

does not allow   allows

....
.... — .... — ....
....

                                  8 .... — ....
7   coating of   ....
.... — ....
cross-section of part of wafer

9   hard   ....

.............—..............   ....—..............

10   11   surface of
                                                      ....

soft   exposed

.............—..............   ....
....

12   13   _____
remaining   addition of

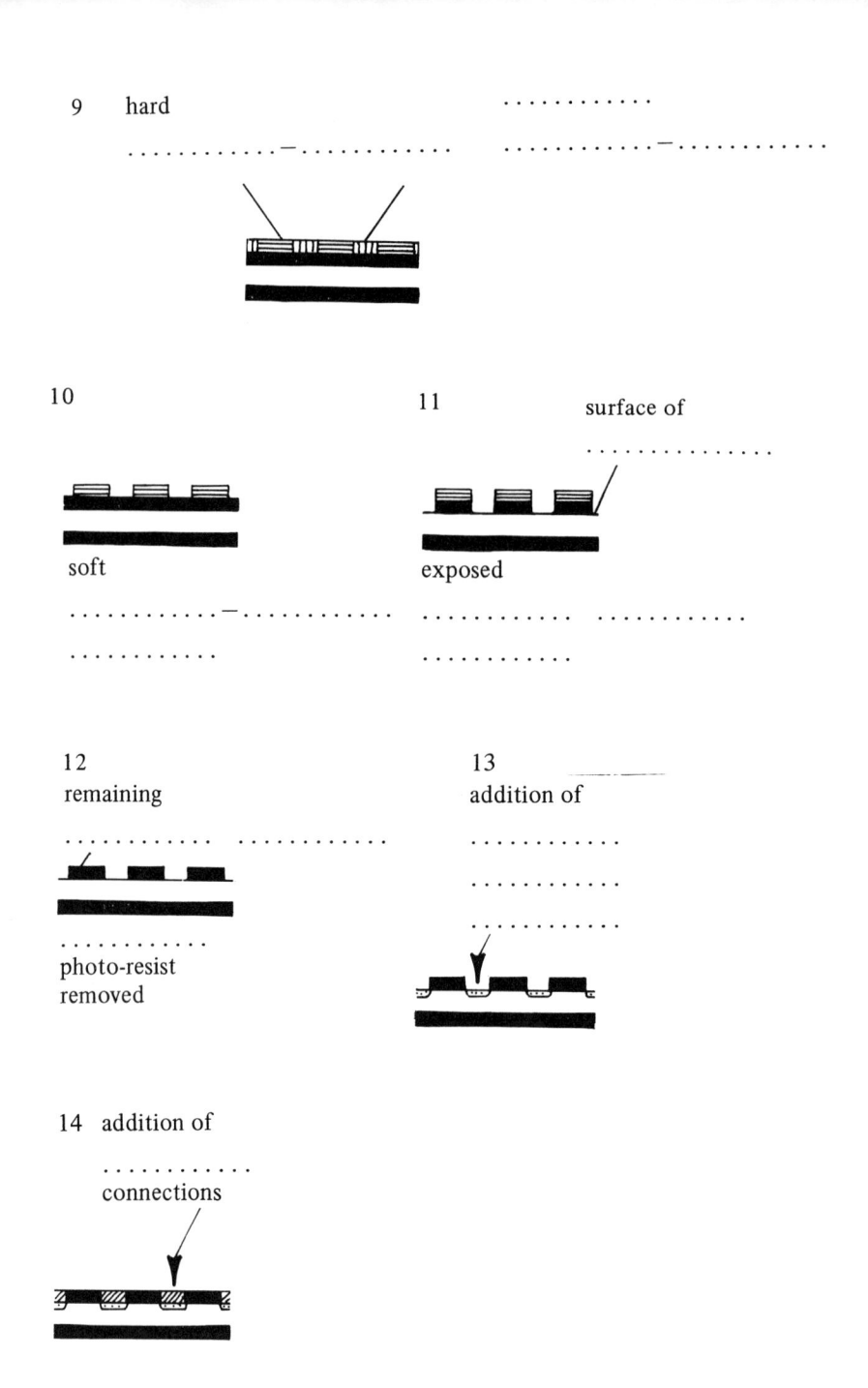

....
                                      ....
                                      ....
....
photo-resist
removed

14   addition of
     ....
     connections

9. Note-making   Make a list of the steps (approx. 19) in the manufacture of a silicon chip. Your steps should be in note form, though you need not use abbreviations. Give only the essential operations and their results; do not explain the reasons for these.

10. Writing   On the basis of 9, above, write a paragraph giving a brief account of the manufacture of a silicon chip.

Unit 7 Rubber

Reading

Pre-read
1. How would you define rubber?
2. Name some of its uses.
3. What does natural rubber come from?
4. How is it obtained?
5. Which parts of the world produce rubber?
6. Rubber is a raw material. Define 'raw material'.
   What raw materials might be required for the construction of:
   a car?
   a sailing boat?
   a house?

Text

Para 1   Fourteenth and fifteenth century travellers to the New World brought back tales to their native Spain and Portugal of a substance marvellous for its resilience and elasticity. The Aztecs used it in their sports, while later reports spoke of its being used to waterproof clothes and shoes. The substance was rubber.

P2   Although rubber has been known from that time, its potential as an industrial material was not appreciated until the eighteen-thirties. Indeed, in the eighteenth century its only use was to erase the marks of pencil on paper. As the East Indies were the principal source of supply at that time, rubber was called 'indiarubber'; the usage has persisted down to these times, although it is now old-fashioned.

P3   Rubber is made from latex, a milky fluid obtained from certain plants and trees which grow in tropical and sub-tropical parts of the world, both in the wild and cultivated in plantations. *Hevea brasiliensis* is probably the most widely-grown rubber tree. The type grown on plantations generally reaches a height of between sixty and eighty feet, but in the wild, specimens have been known to exceed a hundred and twenty-five feet in height, with a girth of eighteen feet.

P4   The latex is actually obtained from the inner bark of the rubber tree. A section of the tree would reveal the heartwood on the inside and a layer of cork bark on the outside. The latex travels through tubes in the soft cortex, but between that and the cork bark is the stone cell layer. There is one other layer, the paper-thin cambium, a vital source of growth for the heartwood next to it and the bark cells on the outer part of the tree.

P5   Latex is extracted by the process of tapping. This involves cutting a diagonal channel in the bark of the trunk at a height of three to four feet from the ground. A small cup is fixed to the trunk, and the latex drains into it along the channel cut into the bark. Normally, *Hevea brasiliensis* is tapped daily or every other day, and tapping cuts are made until ground level is reached.

P6   Tapping must be carried out carefully if it is not to harm the tree. The cut should not extend more than one-third of the way round the trunk, and the channel should run at an angle of 30° to the ground for maximum drainage. There are other methods, however. In certain areas, for instance, planters favour a v-shaped cut. Tapping usually begins when the tree is five to six years old, in the case of the *Hevea*, and continues for another fifteen years, and even, in some cases, another ten years after that.

P7 1 Rubber plantation workers rise early. The latex in the tree flows most freely at dawn, so tapping begins at first light. The latex wells up from that part of the tree below the cut and flows into the collecting cup. The filled cups are emptied into pails and taken back to the collecting point, where they are
5 transferred to larger tanks to await the first processing which will convert the latex juice into raw rubber.

1. Content skim

Read the part of the text indicated *as quickly as possible*, and answer.
1. P1 What is the text about?
2. P2 What other name is rubber known by?
   What was it used for in the eighteenth century?
3. P3 What does latex look like?
4. P4 How many layers cover the heartwood?
5. P5 What is tapping?
6. P6 How many ways of tapping are mentioned?
7. P7 Why do plantation workers get up early?

2. Comprehension scan

Read each statement below and decide, *strictly on the basis of the text*, if it is true (T), false (F), or whether there is insufficient evidence (IE) to decide.

1. The travellers to the New World were Aztecs.
2. The word 'indiarubber' is still used.
3. The industrial potential of rubber was appreciated in the 18th century.
4. Rubber trees are cultivated in parts of the tropics.
5. Cambium is made of paper.
6. Rubber was used to waterproof clothes in the eighteen-thirties.
7. Careless tapping damages a rubber tree.
8. Latex is attracted by sunlight.
9. Some trees can be tapped until they are twenty-five years old.
10. Latex flows from the top to the bottom of the tree.

3. Labelling

Read P4 again, identify each part of the drawing, and label it with the appropriate word from the list.

heartwood
latex tube
cambium
cork bark
cortex
stone cell layer

1
2
3 heartwood
4
5
6

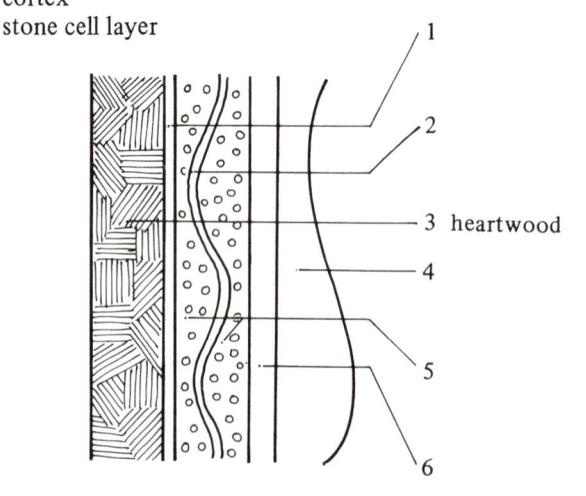

38

4. Controlled note-making

Read P4, 5 and 6 again, completing these notes as you do so. Each space is for one word, abbreviation or symbol.

Tapping

1. Tap. = extract. of ....
   a) diag. chann. cut in trunk .... — ....
      ....
   b) .... fixed trunk

2. Hev. bras. tapped   .... / ....
   ....

3. Method
   a) cut shd. extend ....
      ....
   b) " " = ...
      ....
   c) tap. begins .... / ....
      .... — ....
      ....
   d) " " dawn ∴ ....
      ....
   e) cups empt. into pails, → ....

Listening

5. Decoding

As you listen to Part 1 of the talk, complete the text below.

You ....
how latex is removed from the rubber tree by the simple process of tapping.
Now ....
that latex is converted into the raw rubber which provides the basic material
....
multitude of end products.
But first, what is latex, this ....
..............., milky liquid? Its composition is relatively simple. It
consists chiefly of water. In that water, in solution, ...
.... small amounts of sugars, inorganic salts ....
.... Moving through the liquid by Brownian motion are minute globules
of rubber. When I say 'minute' I am referring to a globule ....

.... of an inch in diameter.

These rubber particles make up a third to two fifths of the weight of the latex, that is to say, they contribute ....

.... of the overall weight of the juice.

6. Sequencing

Listen to the second part of the talk and arrange the sentences below in the correct order by numbering them 1–6.

These additives must be mixed in with the latex within a day of tapping, otherwise it will go sour.
The latex is strained.
It is poured into tanks.
The liquid begins to clot.
The latex is diluted.
Salts or acids are added to the latex.

7. Writing

Using the information in 5 and 6 above, write a paragraph on the processing of latex. The first sentence has been written for you:

To extract rubber from latex, the rubber globules in the juice must be made to coagulate. The first step in the process . . .

8. Guided note-making

Listen to the third part of the talk, taking notes as you do so.

Extracting Rubber from Latex

1. coagulation

2.

3. smoked sheet

4.

9. Sequencing

Using the notes above, complete this flow chart to illustrate the process of rubber extraction.

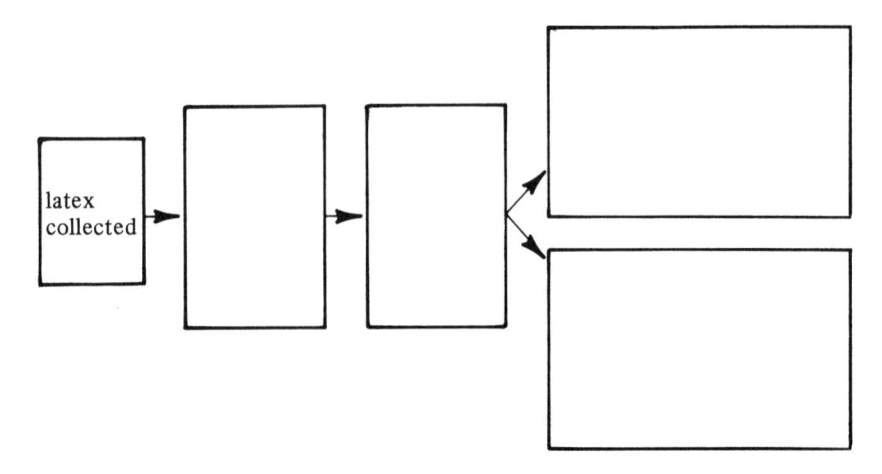

Unit 8

Reading

Pre-read
1. What is a volcano?
2. What happens during an eruption?
3. What famous volcanoes do you know of?
4. What do you know about continental drift?
5. Do you know how continental drift is related to such seismic phenomena as volcanoes and earthquakes?

Text

Para 1
1 Why does the outline of western Africa appear to fit so neatly into that part of the continent of America on the opposite side of the Atlantic? The question was first asked by an English philosopher in 1620. The answer is that some 200 million years ago the continents *did* fit together, and that sub-
5 sequent geological upheavals in the earth's crust have pushed them apart. It is an answer which has been provided by the recent science of plate tectonics, which has begun to explain the phenomenon of continental drift, and the related phenomena of earthquakes and volcanoes.

P2
1 The crust of the earth is divided up, as Fig. 1 illustrates, into six major and many minor zones or plates. These plates 'float' on the earth's mantle, rubbing together along their margins as they do so. Different things happen along different margins. At a *conservative plate margin*, for example, the plates
5 slide alongside each other without any major disturbance being caused.

P3
1 Along a *constructive plate margin*, however, there is considerable activity. The Mid-Atlantic Ridge, a submarine mountain range which runs from the Arctic to the Antarctic, is such a one. Under the oceans the earth's crust is twenty to twenty-two kilometres thinner than the thirty kilometre thick con-
5 tinental crust. It is exceptionally thin, or flawed, along the line of the Mid-Atlantic Ridge, where the heat flow from the centre of the earth is much higher than it is to the sea bed on either side. Below this ridge, molten rock moves by convection from the earth's mantle up through the thin crust. As the semi-liquid rock nears the surface of the oceanic crust, it divides on either
10 side of the ridge, and moves away, creating new crust. The older crust is pushed away from the ridge, and eventually drops back into the mantle at a *destructive plate margin*. Typically, this is a deep ocean trench, such as the Chile-Peru Trench. Over the millions of years in which geological time is measured this process has resulted in the continents drifting in different dir-
15 ections.

P4
1 Volcanoes are a feature of plate margin activity. As the plates rub together, friction is created. This generates heat, which melts some of the rocks of the plates. The molten rock pushes up through the crust and, where it can escape, is erupted in the form of lava and ash. Oceanic volcanoes are found at con-
5 structive plate margins and are formed of basalt lavas. Continental volcanoes are found at destructive plate margins and are formed by lavas of the more complex andesite type. In the talk to follow, this basic division will be extended in a consideration of different forms of volcano, and different types of eruption.

Fig. 1 showing the major zones of the earth's crust.

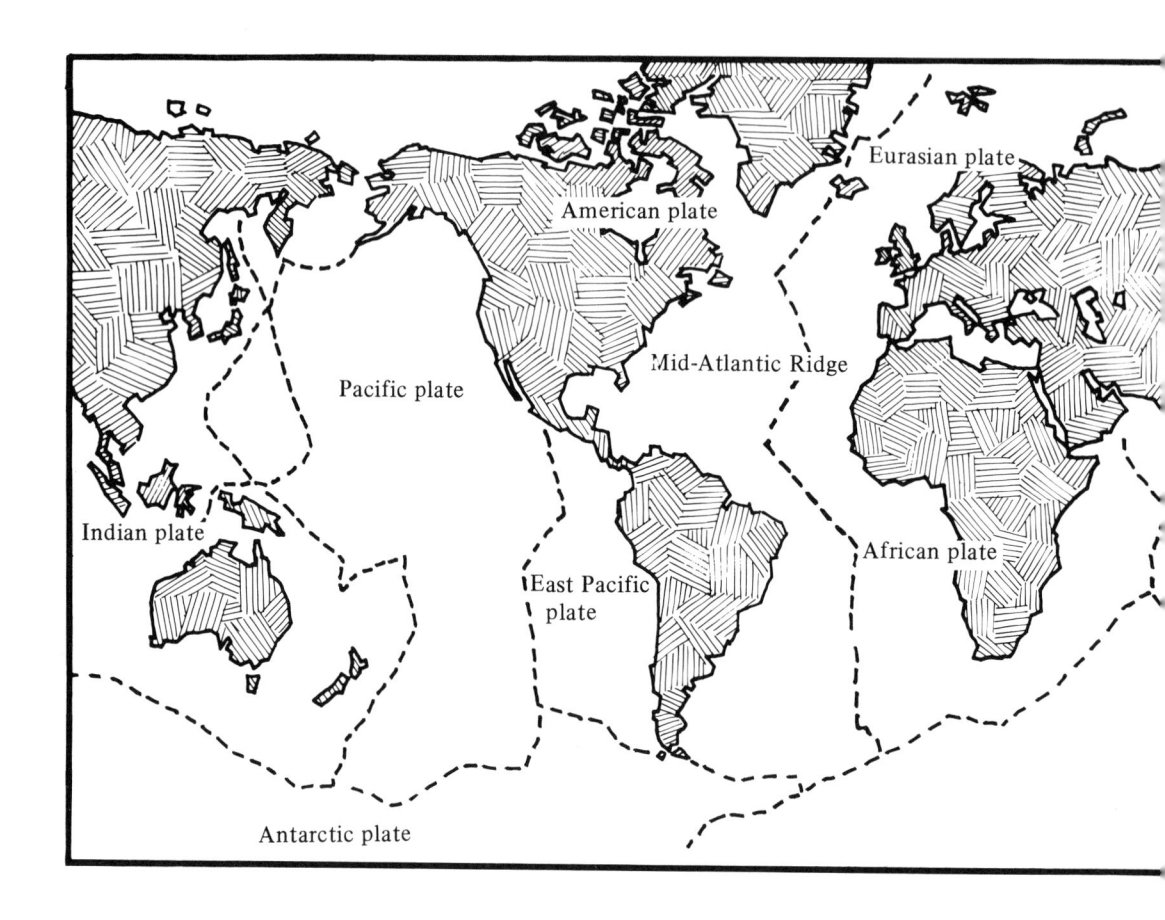

1. Content skim Read the part of the text indicated *as quickly as possible*, and answer.
1. P1 What geological features are explained by the science of plate tectonics?
2. P3 How many types of plate margin are there?
   What are the names of the different types?
3. P4 How many basic types of volcano are there?
   Name them.

2. Comprehension scan Read each statement below and decide, *strictly on the basis of the text*, if it is true (T), false (F), or whether there is insufficient evidence (IE) to decide.
1. Plate tectonics explains the matching shapes of Africa and America.
2. Africa and America have been drifting apart for 200,000,000 years.
3. The crust consists of six plates.
4. There are probably volcanoes on the Mid-Atlantic Ridge.
5. The oceanic crust is 8 – 10 km thick above the earth's mantle.
6. The Mid-Atlantic Ridge is a conservative plate margin.
7. Volcanoes are situated around all types of plate margin.
8. Earthquakes occur around all types of plate margin.
9. Earthquakes are caused by convection currents in the earth's crust.
10. Andesite lavas do not produce oceanic volcanoes.

3. Controlled note-making Read P2, 3 and 4 again, and complete the notes. Each space is for one word, abbreviation or symbol.

Plate Tectonics

Crust = 6 .... + ... min. plates

1. pl. margs. = edges, where pls rub against each other.

2. pl. marg. types:

    a) conserv.

        no ....

    b) construct. e.g. .... − ....
        ....

        i. molt. rock ↗ through ....

        .... by .... ∴ → new

        crust.

        ii. old crust push. ....

        ....

    c) destruct.

        i. old crust disapp. into ....

        ....

        ii. typ. destruct. pl. marg. = ...

        ....

        e.g. .... − ....

        Trench

3. volcanoes:

    a) pls. rub. → ....

    b) .... → ....

    c) heat → rocks ....

    d) molt. rock push. through .... + ...

4. volc. types:

    a) ocean.

        i. found .... pl. ....

        ii. rock = ...

    b) continent.

        i. found .... margs.

        ii. rock = ...

4. Labelling

Read your notes again and complete the diagram below by
   i. labelling: the mid-ocean ridge (constructive plate margin)
                the deep ocean trench (destructive plate margin)
   ii. completing the key by writing against the appropriate
      box: rising mantle convection current
           continental crust
           mantle
           oceanic crust

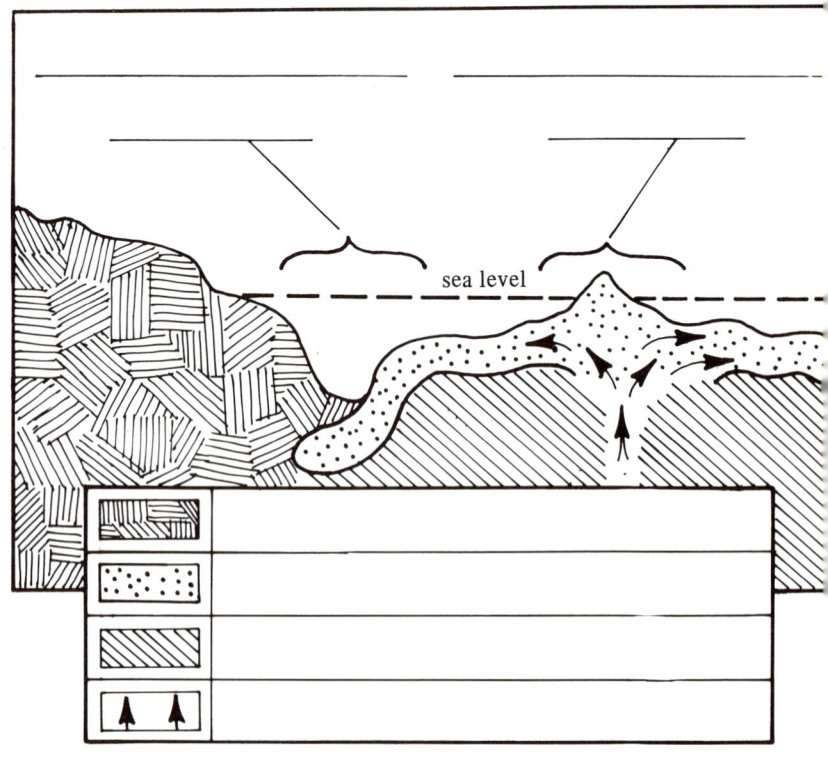

5. Decoding

Listening

As you listen to Part 1 of the talk, complete the text below.

What is a volcano? My dictionary defines it as 'a centre .... of subterranean matter, typically a more or less conical hill or mountain, built ...., with a central crater and pipe'. That's a description which will confirm the image which many of us who do not come from volcanic regions of the world have of a typical volcano, a cone beautiful in ...., and with a wisp of 'smoke' rising from its summit. You and I know that the 'smoke' is no such thing, of course. ...., dust and gases.

But this, of course, is a gross over-simplification. Volcanoes assume many different shapes .... the type of volcanic activity which has constructed them. And they change shape, too. When the Bezymianny Volcano on the Kamchatka Peninsula .... 1955, two hundred metres of the summit ...., and a major part of the side of its crater collapsed. So it's not feasible to try to categorise volcanoes by their shapes. What we can do is postulate different types according to .... eruption on a volcano.

6. Analysing

Listen to Part 2 of the talk. Tick (✓) the features which are found in the different forms of volcanic eruption. Mark non-existent features with a cross (✗). Where a feature is not regularly present, or found in any great quantity, indicate it by a plus sign (+). The analysis of the summit form of eruption has been done for you.

Form of eruption:	*Features:*	Lava from summit	Gas from summit	Lava from vent	Gas from vent	Cone on side	Letter
	Summit	✓	✓	✗	✗	✗	A
	Flank						
	Lateral						
	Parasitic						

45

7. Identifying Now listen to Part 2 of the talk again, check the table above, and identify each of these five outlines as instructed in the talk.

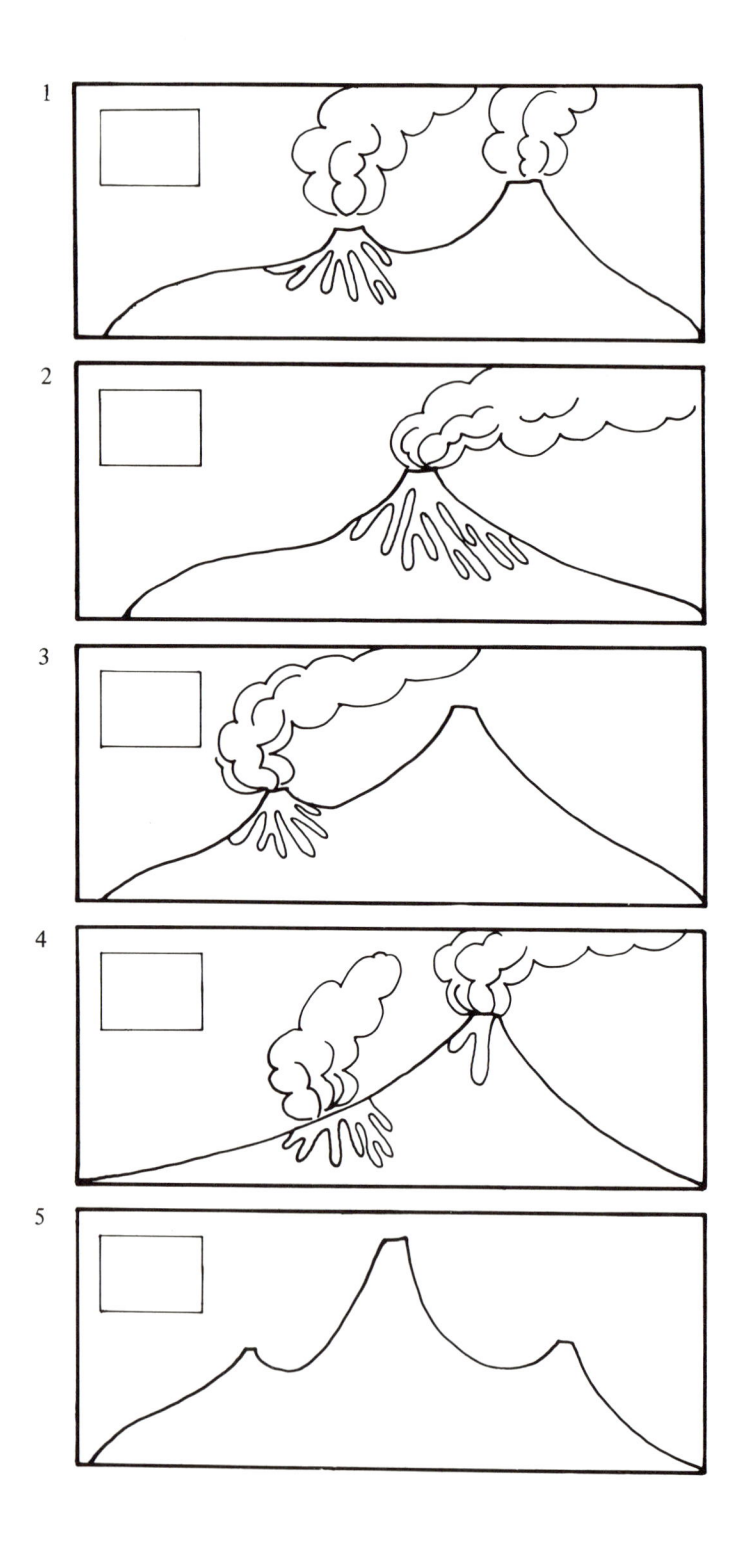

8. Describing

Listen to Part 3 of the talk. As you do, complete the profiles of the different types of eruption by writing short, one or two word, notes in the boxes.

	eruption frequency	lava type	lava heat + fluidity	level of violence	noise level	safety level
Hawaiian	Semi-cont	bas.				
Strombolian						
Vulcanian						

Eruption Profile

9. Classifying

Listen to Part 3 of the talk again, check the notes above, and then read the descriptions of different types of eruption below. Mark the Hawaiian type 'H', the Strombolian 'S', the Vulcanian 'V', and the type not of any of these 'X'.

Mt. Pelée erupted on 8th May, 1902, with disastrous consequences for the inhabitants of the town of St. Pierre below. Part of the dome was blown out, and a great cloud of heated gas escaped sideways and rushed down the mountainsides with the speed of an express train. This was the *nuée ardente*, the 'glowing cloud' which killed tens of thousands. Trees were levelled 24 km from the volcano, and the deposit of ash 9 km away was 30 cm thick. This was an eruption of the most violent type.

Type:

You will stand with the night breeze from the Pacific caressing your hair, watching below you one of nature's miracles. A glowing lake of fire erupting occasionally into magnificent fire fountains as the molten lava shoots high into the air from the surface of the crater-entrapped lava lake. This must surely be nature's finest firework display.

Type:

The terrified villagers pointed at the mountain and cried that it had not spoken since the time of their grandfathers. The volcano exploded noisily and irregularly for weeks, hurling pieces of rock down into the jungle on its slopes. Above it hung a large cloud.

Type:

No sooner had the geological party from Capt. Scott's expedition started to descend Mt Erebus than they heard muted explosions. Small pieces of lava rained around them, and dust, ash and sulphurous fumes rose from the crater behind. Apart from some unpleasant choking and coughing, however, no one suffered any harm.

Type:

Unit 9   Function

Reading

Pre-read

1. How do you give an order in English? Give an example.
2. How do you give an order in your language? Give an example.
3. What points do they have in common? (e.g. structure, length etc.)
4. Make a request and give an invitation in English.
4. Ordering, requesting and inviting are all examples of language *functions*. What do you think a language function is, therefore? Try to devise a definition.

Text

Para 1
1 If ever a children's lib movement were to be formed, its first protest would be against parents' language teaching methods. Consider how the early lessons are taught. At first, the child lies on its back, listening to exclamations about how beautiful it is, how good to finish lunch, how intelligent to grow a
5 second tooth. It is no sooner thoroughly persuaded that it is perfect than stage two begins: orders. 'Stand up! Clever boy!', 'Now take another step! Oh, good girl!' And so on and so forth. But what happens next? As soon as the child begins to show some enthusiasm and initiative to *prove* that it is as clever as its parents have always said, it's 'Don't play with that knife!', 'Stop
10 that noise when your father's sleeping!' and 'Don't put *that* in your mouth!' Child language acquisition is no joke.

P2
1 Like the child learning its mother tongue, most students of a foreign language are exposed to orders, or 'the imperative' at an early stage. There is a certain logic in both cases. Imperatives are generally very simple in structure; reasons are not difficult to surmise. Imperatives carry messages of command, or in-
5 struction, or warning, which act as signposts to guide the individual through the difficulties of a strange environment. Moreover, they often have to be communicated with speed, and therefore the greatest possible economy of utterance. Just as a child has to understand its mother's warning of the risk of playing with matches, it is important for the adult learner in a foreign
10 country to be able to follow, say, a traffic policeman's instructions, to act in a prompt and appropriate manner.

P3
1 So the early parts of the average beginner's course, whether in English or Swahili, feature imperatives. 'Open the window! Close the window!'; the classroom is always too hot, or too cold, at this stage of learning. The windows are opened and closed half a dozen times, to show that 'communication'
5 is taking place. Then the door, by way of variation.

P4
1 In recent years, linguists and language teachers have begun to describe language according not only to *grammatical structure*, using traditional concepts and terms such as the imperative, but also by *function*, that is, the use to which language is put. For example, add 'please' to the order 'Open the win-
5 dow!', and the structure remains imperative. The *function* of the utterance, however, is now that of request, and polite request at that. Function, then, is determined partly by the user's attitude, and is realised by a variety of linguistic and paralinguistic features — vocabulary, grammar and pronunciation, tone of voice, gesture and facial expression. The language learner can often
10 discriminate passively between certain basic functions — those of command

48

and request, for example — although learning to use these different functions of language to communicate effectively is not always so easy. It is the learner's failure to master a sufficient number of the components of a function that causes chauvinists the world over to complain of the 'rudeness' of foreigners, when the last thing the unfortunate foreigner intended was to be impolite.

P5 1 Function is also determined by the situation in which the language is used. 'Be quiet!' coming from a teacher tired of noisy pupils is obviously an order, or command. Used by one nervous bank robber to a fellow in crime, when he thinks he has heard a noise which could have been made by a suspicious policeman, the sentence would be a warning. Used again, as they prepare to blow open the safe, its function would be that of cautioning; too loud an explosion would give them away. Look at 'the imperative' in this way, then, and we realise that it consists of a small set of structural forms which can fulfil many different functions: commands, prohibitions, warnings, exhortations, as well as many others.

P6 1 To sum up, the approach to the study and use of language through the examination of its functions has been enriching for teachers and learners alike. For both, of course, the functional approach does not dispense with the need for attention to be paid to the workings of the grammar of a language, but it is an approach which extends the uses to which the control of structure may be put.

1. Content skim

Read the part of the text indicated *as quickly as possible*, and answer.
1. P4 What is the passage about?
2. P1 What does the writer mean by saying 'Child language acquisition is no joke'?
3. P2 Why are imperatives important to children and language learners at an early stage?
4. P4/5 What two things determine language function?
5. P5 What four functions are mentioned which may be fulfilled by the imperative?
6. Can you give an example of each of these four functions? 'Stand up!', for example, is a command.

2. Comprehension scan

Read each statement below and decide, *strictly on the basis of the text*, if it is true (T), false (F), or whether there is insufficient evidence (IE) to decide.
1. Imperatives are short because they are often said slowly.
2. Parents react negatively when their children show initiative.
3. Only English and Swahili beginners' courses teach imperatives.
4. English and Swahili have the same imperative structures.
5. Adding 'please' to 'Open the window' does not change the structure of the utterance.
6. Language function is a traditional concept.
7. Some English people think foreigners are rude because often they do not use English in the proper way.
8. The functional approach to language teaching has made language teachers wealthy.
9. A knowledge of grammar is less essential than it used to be.
10. Language function is partly the result of how the speaker feels towards his or her subject or listener.

3. Guided note-making

Study the sets of functions below. Make sure that you understand the meaning of each function, and how it differs from the others. Then decide which function each group 1–10 below contains examples of.

Ordering	Telling someone to do something
	e.g. Go away!
Warning	Telling someone of possible danger
	e.g. Look out!
Cautioning	Advising of possible adverse consequences
	e.g. Don't eat so fast or you'll be sick.
Inviting	e.g. Come to dinner tomorrow.
Offering	e.g. Take my seat.
Suggesting	e.g. Let's go for a walk.
Requesting	e.g. Open the window, please.
Instructing	Telling someone how to do something
	e.g. First, break two eggs.
Exhorting	Giving strong support and encouragement
	e.g. Come on, Scotland!
Prohibiting	Telling someone not to do something
	e.g. No smoking.

Note that not all of the forms are imperative in structure.

Group 1
Sit still!
Be patient!
Come over here!
Stop, look and listen.

Group 2
Knock him down Ali!
Shoot!

Group 3
Come up and see me sometime.
Drop in for a chat if you're passing.
Call round any time.

Group 4
Thin ice.
Danger. Men working overhead.
These premises are patrolled by guard dogs.
Take care!

Group 5
Let's watch that comedy programme.
How about going to the cinema?
What about steak for dinner?

Group 6
Take my coat. It'll keep you warm.
Have another piece of cake.
Borrow my umbrella if you like.

Group 7
Hold this for a moment, will you?
Give me a hand please.
Turn the TV down, won't you?

Group 8
Do not speak to the driver while the vehicle is in motion.
No entry.
Walking on the grass is prohibited.

Group 9
See that you don't drive through the lights again.
Be more careful in future.

Group 10
Lift the receiver.
Listen for the dialling tone.

4. Decoding

Listening

As you listen to Part 1 of the talk, complete the text below.

In our everyday life, we are surrounded by instructions; .... that we fail to realise just how many, and just how automatic is our response to most of them. There are differences in content and form, of course. Some .... than others; it is safe to ignore some, but not others.

.... for a moment how my day begins, and probably yours too. .... to work by car, I am bombarded by commands in the form of coloured lights, signs, symbols and numerals. If I go by train, ... to show my ticket, ... I can smoke, not to stick my head out of the window. When I arrive at College, a notice tells me that I must show my identity card to get in.

.... of simple instructions; notice, by the way, that I have been using 'instruction' ...., in the idiomatic way, to mean the same as 'order'. .... telling someone how to do something that was our earlier, stricter, definition, it brings us back to the idea of instruction .... sequential orders, often given with reasons. Recipes tell us how to cook and bake, patterns to knit and sew, maps how to get from A to B. .... gadget we buy, from a tin-opener to a micro-computer, comes complete with instructions we .... make the equipment function properly. So being able to follow (and give) instructions is vital. And since the function of instructing is often realised by imperatives, you are now going to be given a couple of exercises in following instructions.

51

5. Following instructions Listen to Part 2 of the talk and follow the instructions.

Fig. 1

6. Following instructions Listen to Part 3 of the talk and follow the instructions.

Fig. 2

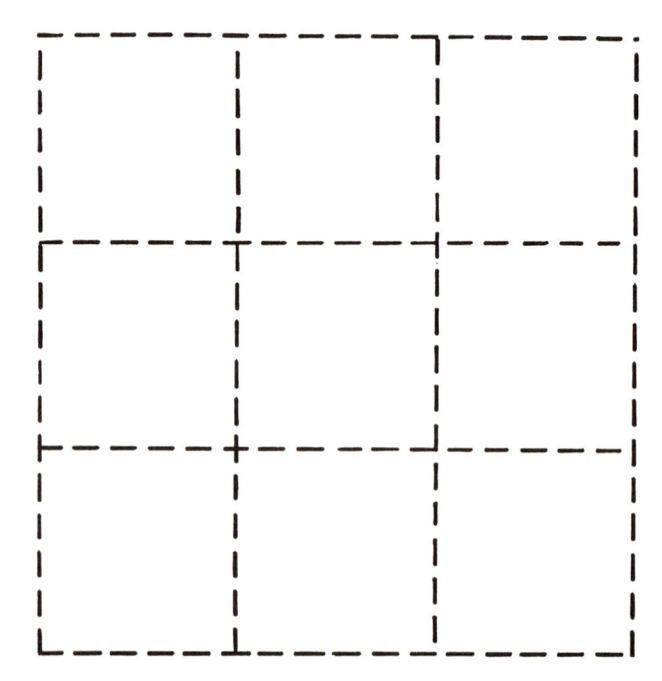

Unit 10   Kalahari Bushmen

Reading

Pre-read
1. What do you associate with deserts?
2. What sorts of people live in deserts? How do they obtain their living?
3. What do you know about the Kalahari Desert?
4. What do you understand by the term 'natural man'? How does 'natural man' live?
5. How do peoples who are 'hunter-gathers' live?
6. How many examples of 'hunter-gatherer' peoples can you give?

Text

Para 1
1 Few of the peoples of the world can come closer in their life styles to that of Rousseau's 'natural man' than the Bushmen of the Kalahari Desert. Their society is non-materialistic and caring; their way of life is perfectly attuned to their environment; and the Bushmen are a gentle and peace-loving people.
5 The Kalahari Desert of southern Africa extends over 260,000 square kilometres, mostly of Botswana. The term 'desert' is something of a misnomer, for although the region has no permanent standing water and has areas of sand dunes, it is actually a rolling, sandy plain, covered in the main by scrub, grasses and trees. It is also rich in wildlife. Summer temperatures soar to over
10 50°C, while during winter nights they may fall to as low as −7°C. The average annual rainfall may be as high as 46 cm in the eastern part of the Kalahari basin, but in the south-west it is less than half of that.

P2
1 Life, on the face of it, would appear to be harsh for a people living in such an environment. Yet the !Kung (the ! indicates the initial click sound of their name) who inhabit the area now contained within the Central Kalahari Game Reserve rank eleventh in the world in terms of daily protein intake. The
5 !Kung of this region still pursue the traditional way of life of hunter-gatherers. From their superficially inhospitable environment they kill enough warthog, wildebeest and antelope (to name only three of the animals which they hunt) to provide a kilo of meat per day for every member of the group. The other two thirds of their daily protein intake is provided by the 34 types of edible
10 plant which are gathered. Most important of these is the high-protein mangetti nut, the fruit of a prolific shrub, hardened to drought conditions and which can remain fresh, on the ground, for twelve months.

P4
1 Like many natural peoples, the !Kung organise the methods by which they obtain their food on the basis of sex. By and large it is the women who are the gatherers. Groups of between three and five will scour an area within an 8 km radius of the camp for such plants as the mangetti, baobab fruits and
5 the wild melon which is sometimes the only source of water during droughts. The men go hunting, singly or in pairs, generally travelling between 12 and 24 km from their camp. Their weapon is a small bow which fires an unfeathered arrow over a short distance. The secret of their success lies in their stalking ability, and in the poison, extracted from desert grubs, with which
10 the tips of their arrows are coated. This poison will kill an animal within twelve hours, and then dissipate, so that the meat can be eaten in perfect safety. Both men and women can obtain food in these ways in an average 'working' week of fourteen hours.

P5   1 The gentle Bushpeople live in bands 5—16 families strong, which are constantly on the move; on average, a site is occupied for 3—4 weeks. The bands frequently change in composition. When a dispute arises between individuals or families in the band, there is generally a truce for a few days, and then one
5 or other of the opponents leaves. Bands have usually split up into family groups by mid-winter, in the middle of August, each family fending for itself. The arrival of the six-month summer in November sees bands re-forming. Because the Bushpeople are nomadic, perhaps, they have developed remarkably little sense of individual possession. An individual's 'property' rarely
10 exceeds 20 kg in weight. And the utensils, weapons and ornaments which make that up will be loaned without hesitation. Not only is property shared, but food also. The Bushmen allow no member of their society to go in want, and the old are especially well looked-after. A Bushmen hunter, for example, allocates part of his share of a successful hunt first to his father and mother-
15 in-law, next to his own parents, and only after that, to his own wife and children.

P6   1 Those of us who belong to 'advanced' societies could learn much to our advantage from the philosophy and practices of such natural peoples as the Bushmen of the Kalahari.

1. Content skim

Read the part of the text indicated *as quickly as possible* and answer.
1. P2 Is the Kalahari a real desert?
2. P3 What sort of people are the !Kung?
3. P4 How do the !Kung divide the labour of obtaining food?
4. P5 How do members of the band deal with arguments?
5. P5/6 What lessons, in your opinion, could our societies draw from the Bushmen?

2. Comprehension scan

Read each statement below and decide, *strictly on the basis of the text*, if it is true (T), false (F), or whether there is insufficient evidence (IE) to decide.
1. Average annual rainfall increases westward across the Kalahari.
2. Only ten peoples in the world have a higher daily protein intake than the !Kung.
3. One third of their daily protein intake comes from meat.
4. The !Kung eat an average of 2 kg of plants per day.
5. The mangetti is an extremely nutritious fruit.
6. Lack of water causes the mangetti to become hard.
7. !Kung men do not gather plants.
8. !Kung hunters are lightly armed.
9. The Kalahari 'summer' lasts from November until June.
10. Desert grubs must be dangerous to eat.

3. Matching

Each sentence in Group B is the consequence of one sentence in Group A. Match the sentences.

Group A

1. Food is plentiful in the Kalahari and easily obtained by the Bushmen.
2. The !Kung bow and arrow has a very limited range.
3. The poison disappears after twelve hours.
4. For most of the year there is no standing water in the Kalahari.
5. The mangetti nut is tough, durable and rich in protein.
6. The Kalahari is rich in vegetation and wildlife.
7. The !Kung are nomads.
8. There are 34 edible plant species in the Kalahari.

9. The !Kung willingly lend any of their possessions.
10. They are a peaceful people who share their property and care for everyone.

Group B

11. Water-bearing fruit such as melon are very important.
12. The meat is safe to eat.
13. The !Kung need not 'work' more than a fourteen-hour week.
14. It is not a desert like the Sahara.
15. They carry only a light load.
16. We could benefit by imitating certain of their ways.
17. The arrows have to be poisoned.
18. They have not developed in real sense of private ownership.
19. It forms an important part of the !Kung diet.
20. The vegetable diet of the !Kung is varied.

4. Writing

Now combine the sentences to show the relationship of consequence. Use the following markers:

Initial   **Middle**
Since . . .   . . . so . . .
                    . . . so that . . .
As . . .   . . . with the result that . . .
                    . . . (and) because of this . . .

Example

Since the poison disappears after twelve hours, the meat is safe to eat.

As

The poison disappears after twelve hours	so / and because of this	
The poison disappears after twelve hours,	so that / with the result that	the meat is safe to eat.
The poison disappears after twelve hours;	because of this	

Listening

5. Controlled note-making

Listen to Part 1 of the talk and complete the notes.

Paralanguage

1. ParaL. = syst. . . . . - . . . . commun.

    i.e. . . . . + sounds replace . . . .

2. Nat. ParaL. = a) extend L.

    b) subst. for L. when circs. ≠ . . . .

    . . . .

3. main types:

    a) commun. at . . . .

                i. using body - e.g. ....
                ii. "   sound - e.g. whistle .... of
                        ....
         b) commun. in ....
                i. import. for e.g. ....
         c) comp. L. i.e. emphasize or .... speech.
                e.g. wink = ...
                        ....

6. Decoding

Listen to Part 2 of the talk and fill in the gaps in the transcript. Each space is for one word, abbreviation or symbol.

While paralanguage .... universal, ... differences in its forms across cultures. In Western societies, for example, a person who wishes .... signal 'Come here!' will .... his or her forefinger, or cup a hand with the fingers upward, and move it towards the body. In certain Near and Far Eastern societies the hand is cupped also, but with the fingers pointing downwards. Confusion may .... between members of these different cultures, as the 'Come here!' gesture in which the fingers point down looks remarkably like the gesture which indicates 'Go away!' to ....

.... counting on the fingers also .... A Western person will strike each finger of one hand with the forefinger of the other as the numbers .... counted. This is also found in many countries of the Middle and Near East, ... so is the method in which the thumb of one hand is .... against each finger of that hand, finishing with the thumb placed .... the centre of the .... on the count of five.

7. Identifying

Listen to Part 2 of the talk again and identify the fingers of the hand.

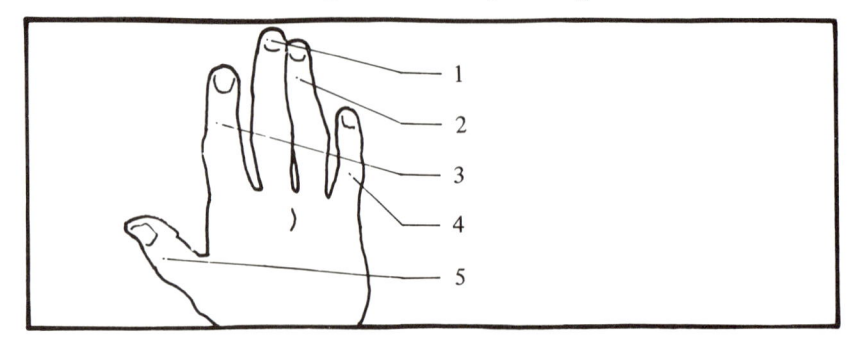

8. Classifying

Listen to Part 3 of the talk and decide which type (A–F) each picture is of. Then, listen to the last part of Part 3 again and (from the list below) write in the name of the animal which the sign represents.

hawk / ostrich / hare / porcupine / giraffe / lion

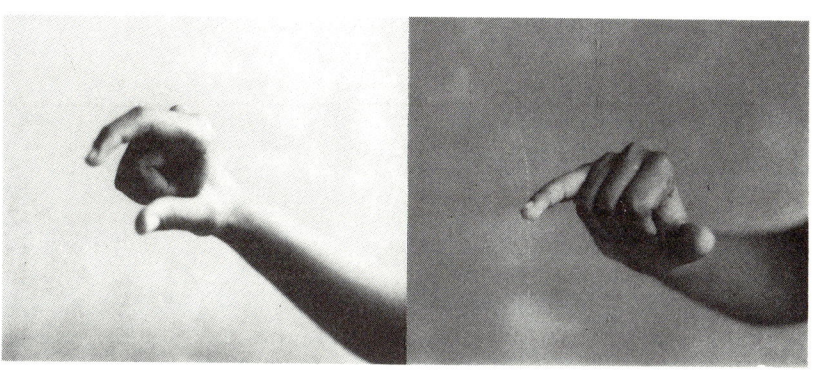

Type:
Animal:

Type:
Animal:

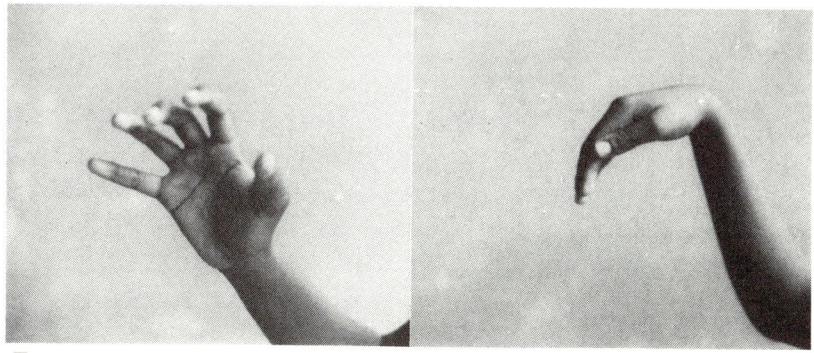

Type:
Animal:

Type:
Animal:

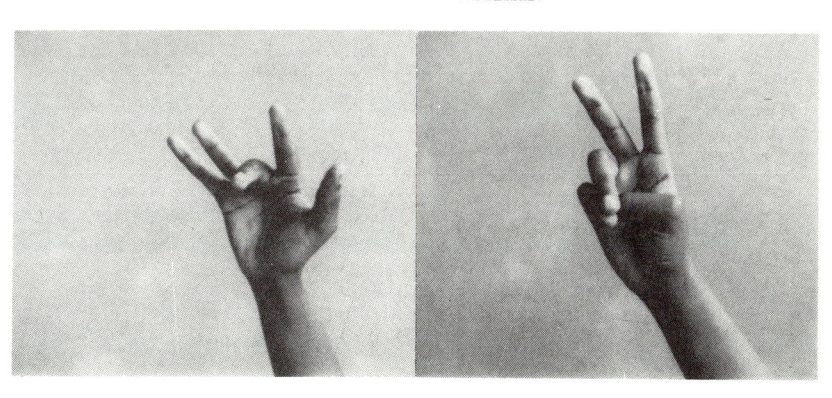

Type:
Animal:

Type:
Animal:

Unit 11   The Camera

Reading

Pre-read

1. What different types of camera are there?
2. What are the most important parts of a camera?
3. How does a camera work?
4. What are the basic rules of good photography?

1 Set the Camera to "MANUAL" for Film Loading

Turn the Aperture Ring to set any F number against the red line in front of the Viewfinder. Now the shutter can be released regardless of light conditions.

2 Open the Rear Cover and Load Film

Pull out the Rear Cover Lock to open. Then pull up the Rewind Knob, place the cartridge in the Film Compartment and push the Rewind Knob back.

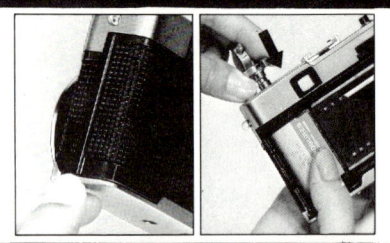

3 Engage Film with the Take-up Spool

Slot the film leader into the Take-up Spool. Advance the film using the wind-on wheel. Make sure film perforations engage on both sides. Close the Rear Cover tightly. Take up any slack in film by turning the Rewind Crank clockwise.

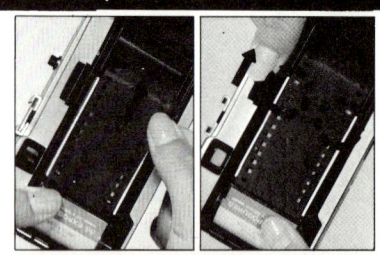

4 Advance Film to "1"

Keep winding film and releasing the shutter until the Film Counter points to "1". The Rewind Knob should rotate to show the film is being advanced properly.

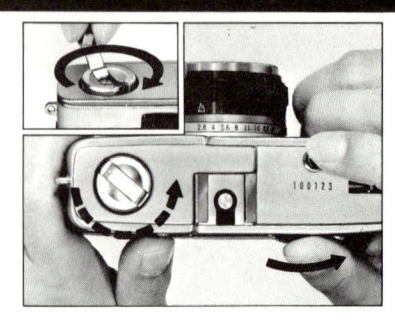

5 Set ASA Film Speed

Turn ASA Setting Ring until ASA number of the film being used appears in the ASA Window.

6 Switch the Camera to "AUTOMATIC"

Turn Aperture Ring until "A" mark is aligned with the red line in front of the viewfinder (click stop).

7 Focusing

Estimate the subject distance and set appropriate zone symbol against the red line by turning the Focusing Ring. For general picture taking, set the group-snap symbol (👥), which gives a good result. The Symbol Checking Window lets you set the symbol while looking through the viewfinder. For critical focusing (and flash photography) use the scale (m, ft) engraved on the lower part of focusing ring: simply set the subject distance against a red line there.

(Note: The focusing ring does not rotate 360°.)

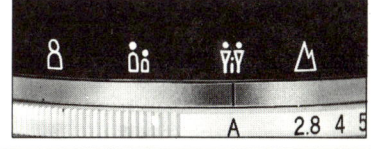

8 Compose and Release the Shutter

Compose within the bright frame. Hold the camera firmly and press the Shutter Release Button with the ball of index finger. When taking close-ups, frame the subject within 3 small parallax marks. If the subject is too dim, the shutter release locks and a red flag enters viewfinder: select a brighter subject or use a flash unit.

9 Rewind the Film

When the last frame is exposed, DO NOT attempt to advance the film; the Film Counter may point to 36, 20 or 12 depending upon the length of film used. Press the Rewind Button on the baseplate. Fold out the Rewind Crank and turn it in the direction of the arrow until the film is completely rewound. Open the Rear Cover, pull up the Rewind Knob and remove the cartridge.

1. Content skim

Read the part of the text indicated *as quickly as possible*, and answer.
1. P1–P9 How many stages must be completed before the first photo can be taken?
2. P7 How many general distance settings does the camera have?
3. P8 What indicates that a flash should be used?
4. P9 What is the maximum number of photographs that can be taken on one film?

2. Comprehension scan

Read each statement below and decide, *strictly on the basis of the text*, if it is true (T), false (F), or whether there is insufficient evidence (IE) to decide.
1. When the camera is set at 'Manual' it is always possible to release the shutter.
2. The camera cannot be loaded when it is set on 'Automatic'.
3. If the rewind knob is not turning, the film is not being properly advanced.
4. The film does not stop while being wound on to '1'.
5. For general picture taking, the distance setting should be used.
6. The focusing ring comes off if rotated 360°.
7. Lack of sufficient available light locks the shutter release.
8. If an attempt is made to advance the film after the last frame has been exposed, the film will be damaged.
9. The film rewinds automatically after the final exposure.
10. Pressing the shutter release button with the thumb is inadvisable.

3. Controlled note-making

Read P1–4 again, completing the notes as you do so. Use the following abbreviations in your note-making. Each space is for one word, abbreviation or symbol.

VF	Viewfinder	WOW	Wind-on Wheel
RCL	Rear Cover Lock	RC	Rear Cover
RK	Rewind Knob	RCr	Rewind Crank
TS	Take-up Spool	FC	Film Counter

Loading the film

1. .... Man.
    a) .... apert. ring to any ....
        .... against red line ....
        .... VF.
2. .... rear cov.
3. .... film
    a) .... out RCL
    b) .... up RK + insert ....
    c) .... back
4. .... film
    a) slot f. in ....
    b) .... f. by ....
    c) close ....
    d) take up slack – turn ....
5. .... film

a) wind f. + ... shut. till FC . . . .
. . . .
b) check RK . . . .

4. Giving instructions

Imagine that a friend of yours who is not a very good photographer is looking through the viewfinder of the camera. The scenes which your friend sees are shown below. React to what your friend says by giving the most appropriate instructions from this list.

a) Don't point it at the sun!
b) Use the flash!
c) Frame her inside the parallax marks!
d) Set it on the distant symbol!
e) You'll have to stand further back!
f) Move the focusing ring to the group snap symbol.

1. It's awfully bright!

2. The mountains look terribly far away!

3. Her head seems awfully close.

4. Nothing's happened!

5. What focus should this have?

6. I've got nearly all of her in, but not quite.

61

5. Labelling

Listening

Listen to Part 1 of the talk and label the pieces of equipment, using the names of the different items given below.

clips   beaker   thermometer
rubber tube and filter   timer   developing tank

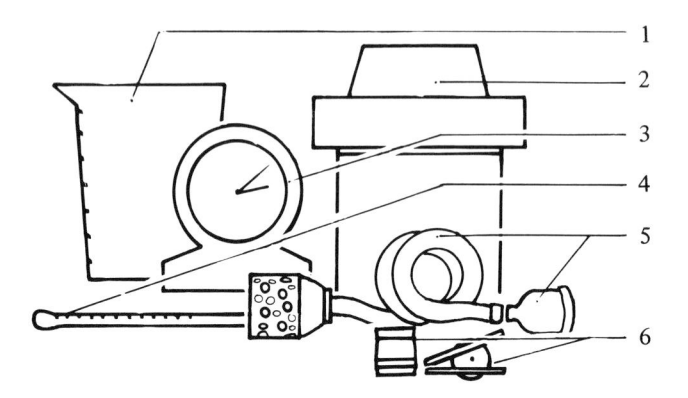

6. Decoding

As you listen to Part 1 of the talk, complete the text below.

This afternoon we are going to find out how to develop an ordinary black and white film. So first we'll look at what we need — what equipment and chemicals, I mean — and after that look at each step in the process. Remember, we're only talking about developing photographic film. Printing the photographs will come later.

So first of all, ...
....................? Well, this is the equipment here. As I'm showing it, you write in the names of the pieces against the illustrations which you've got .... you. We'll start with the developing tank, which is where most of the action takes place: that's where we put the film and the chemicals. ....
.... on my left is a stainless steel tank. It's dear compared to the plastic type, but it'll last much longer. Here, on my right, that's your left, of course, ...
.... couple of measuring instruments. There's a thermometer, ...
.... in black and white development it's important to keep the chemicals' temperature on twenty degrees centigrade. Then this here is a timer. I find it easier to see than my watch. That beaker behind it is a measurer too — ....
measure our chemicals out accurately. Finally, a rubber tube and water filter

to wash the film after ....

.... the chemicals, and, oh yes, these at the very front are clips, used to hang the film up to dry. I like this plastic sort myself, because they don't go rusty like your metal ones.

Well, that's the hardware; ....

.... chemicals? We only need three. The developer — it's an alkaline solution — comes in powder form, so we've got to add water. You can get it as .... ,

but it's much dearer that way, so my advice is, don't bother. The stop bath is

.... ,

which means it stops the developer's action straight away, and that helps to guard against over-development. Last, there's the fixer, which fixes or sets the film.

7. Sequencing

Listen to Part 2 of the talk. Number the steps below (which are given in the order in which you hear them) in the correct order for the procedure of developing a film. The first step has been identified for you; number the remainder 2 to 6.

Number

.... The tank is loaded.

.... The film is put into the reel.

......1...... The film is removed from the cassette and peeled from the backing paper.

.... The temperature of the chemicals is checked.

.... The developer is poured in quickly.

.... The timer is started.

8. Writing

Now write up the first six steps in the development of a black and white film as a set of instructions, using the same form as is used in the first instruction below.
1. Remove the film from the cassette and peel it from the backing paper.

9. Guided note-making

Listen to Part 3 of the talk and complete the notes as you do so.

Devel. B + W film (cont.)

1. Shake tank

        a)

        b)

2. Pour

3. " in

4. Shake

5. Pour

6. " in

7.

8.

9.

10. Writing

Using the information in 5, 7 and 9 write a description of how a black and white film is developed. Divide the text into a section on equipment and one on process. Each section has been started for you. Make sure that you follow the style and structures.

Developing a black and white film

Equipment
developing tank
beaker
. . .

Method
The first step in the development of the film is its removal from the cassette. Next, the film is peeled away from its backing paper. The temperature of the chemicals is then checked — it should be 20°C. Once this has been done, the tank . . .

Unit 12   Pliny and Pompeii

Reading

Pre-read
1. What do you know about Vesuvius?
2. What happens during a volcanic eruption?
3. What happened to Pompeii?
4. What is there to see in present-day Pompeii?

Text

Para 1   1 At daybreak on 26th August, 79 A.D., a search party was picking its way along the shore at Stabiae on the Bay of Naples in southern Italy. Suddenly one of the men gave a shout, and when his companions had run up he pointed out the body of a stout, well-dressed man, looking more asleep than dead.

P2   1 The body was that of Pliny the Elder, who had achieved fame among fellow Romans as a historian. The scholar was a man of action too, and at the time of his death was commander of the naval fleet at Misenum, farther round the bay.

P3   1 Two days before he was discovered, Vesuvius had exploded in the catastrophic eruption which submerged the thriving towns of Pompeii and Herculaneum under a sea of ash and mud. When the first signs of volcanic activity had become evident, and a great plume in the shape of an umbrella pine tree
      5 hung above the volcano, the admiral decided to go from Misenum by ship to obtain a better view. He invited his nephew, known to us as the Younger Pliny, but the young man declined.

P4   1 Pliny's scientific expedition was not to be, however, for before he had embarked, he received a message at about 2 p.m. from friends with a house at the foot of the mountain, begging for his help. Pliny set off on this rescue attempt to the area where Torre del Greco stands today, but was unable to
      5 land because access to the beach was prevented by volcanic debris. By this time, ash, pumice and blackened stones were falling on and all around the ship.

P5   1 That night was spent at the home of Pomponanius, another friend. Having abandoned his rescue effort, Pliny had set sail for his friend's house at Stabiae, further round the Bay again. He found Pomponanius desperately trying to evacuate his household by ship, but unable to do so because of the on-
      5 shore wind.

P6   1 The Elder Pliny attempted to calm the fears of his friend and his family, and persuaded them all to return to the house. Here he had a bath, dined and went to bed. We know from the letter of his nephew to Tacitus, the historian, that he slept well, for his snoring was commented upon.

P7   1 Sometime the following morning, conditions had deteriorated so much that Pliny was awakened and began to make his way down to the shore with his hosts. Although day had broken, it was so dark that torches had to be lit, and the danger from falling debris was so great that the members of the party
      5 had tied pillows round their heads in an effort to avoid injury by falling stones.

P8   1 Pliny began to show signs of physical distress on the way to the beach. He lay down for a time, and repeatedly asked for water. Finally, the inferno of flames and sulphur fumes forced the others to flee, leaving the exhausted Pliny leaning on two slaves for support. Quite suddenly, he collapsed, becom-

65

5 ing the most famous victim of the eruption. Opinion is divided as to whether he was suffocated by the fumes or died of a heart attack, but it now seems probable that the former is the less likely cause.

1. Content skim

Read the part of the text indicated *as quickly as possible*, and answer.
1. P3 What natural disaster is described?
2. P3 What did the Elder Pliny decide to do?
3. P5 What prevented Pomponanius from sailing?
4. P6 How did Pliny react to the dangers of the eruption?
5. P8 What signs of illness did Pliny show?

2. Comprehension scan

Read each statement below and decide, *strictly on the basis of the text*, if it is true (T), false (F), or whether there is insufficient evidence (IE) to decide.
1. The Younger Pliny was afraid to go with his uncle.
2. The Elder Pliny was still alive when he was found.
3. Torre del Greco stands at the foot of Vesuvius.
4. The site of Stabiae is closer to modern Torre del Greco than it is to Misenum.
5. Pliny the Younger did not survive the eruption.
6. The Younger Pliny was probably known by that name to his contemporaries.
7. A north wind prevented Pomponanius from sailing.
8. The eruption made the beach at Torre del Greco inaccessible from the sea.
9. Pliny did not sleep soundly on the first night of the eruption.
10. Pliny was alone when he died.
11. There are two schools of thought as to the cause of his death.
12. He probably died of suffocation.

3. Sequencing

Put the sentences below in chronological order. Give the dates.

A. The eruption of Vesuvius was seen from Misenum.
B. They went down to the beach.
C. Ash, pumice and blackened stones were falling.
D. They went back to his house.
E. The Elder Pliny received a call for help from a friend.
F. He set sail for his friend's house at the foot of the mountain.
G. However, the wind prevented him.
H. His companions stayed for a while, then ran from the fumes.
I. The ship was unable to land.
J. It sailed on to Stabiae.
K. Another friend, Pomponanius, was trying to launch a ship from there.
L. He collapsed suddenly.
M. Conditions worsened further and Pliny was awakened.
N. Pliny bathed and went to bed.
O. The members of the party lit torches.
P. Pliny began to feel ill, lay down and kept asking for water.
Q. His body was discovered two days after the eruption.

4. Writing

Now, tell the story in a piece of continuous narrative writing.
a) decide which of the sentences should be combined.
b) make the combinations, with the necessary structural changes and using such markers as:

when	next	however
while	the following	therefore
after (that)	subsequently	
	finally	

Write three paragraphs, one for each day described in the text.
Begin: After the eruption of Vesuvius was first seen from Misenum, the Elder Pliny received a call for help from a friend.

5. Transferring information

Complete the map by following the instructions and using the information given.

Show the following:

towns by writing and underlining the name beside the appropriate black circle;

e.g. ● *Misenum*

Vesuvius by drawing lines radiating from the appropriate black circle and naming it;

i.e. ✸ *Vesuvius*

Pliny the Elder's route, using a broken line;

i.e. — — — — —

the wind direction off Stabiae using broken arrows;

i.e.   --→--→--→

the points of the compass writing N for North, S for South, E for East and W for West.

Information:

Misenum is the most northerly town on the Bay of Naples.
Vesuvius stands about half-way round the Bay, its crater about 10 km inland.
Stabiae lies almost due south of Misenum, on the other side of the Bay.
Pompeii is the town nearest Stabiae, just north of the River Sarnus.
Herculaneum is further round the Bay, the town nearest Misenum.
Torre del Greco lies between Pompeii and Herculaneum.

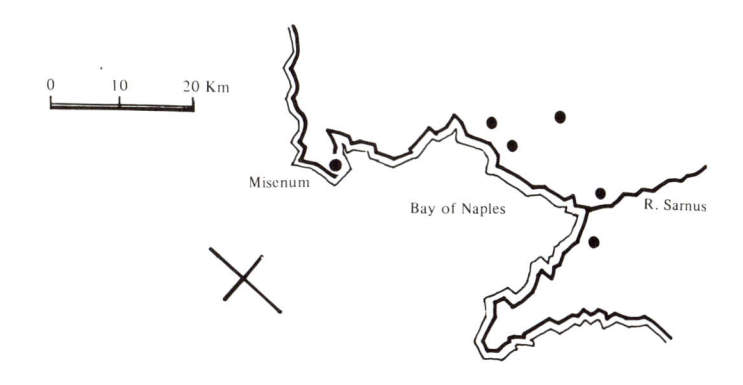

67

Listening

6. Defining

Listen to Part 1 of the talk and as you do, fill in the English half of the Latin-English glossary below.

Latin		English
Alae	=	
Atrium	=	
Fauces	=	
Peristylum	=	
Tablinum	=	
Triclinium	=	
Vestibulum	=	

7. Decoding

As you listen to Part 1 of the talk again, complete the text below.

The houses of well-to-do families in Pompeii and Herculaneum varied in size, number of rooms and layout, but nevertheless displayed many features in common. A typical house of the first century B.C. consisted of .... only, but had an area of, say ....

Outside, the roof was generally flat, and the walls brightly painted. The walls were blank, windowless, except possibly for some small windows in the sides, but .... flanked the doors.

Like traditional houses in the Middle East today, the houses were inward-looking. The main entrance was .... divided by a door. The outer part of the corridor was the vestibulum, V-E-S-T-I-B-U-L-U-M, which has given us the English ...., still in use today; the inner vestibule was the fauces, F-A-U-C-E-S. At the end of the fauces the house .... a hall open to the sky. In the centre of this hall, the atrium, that's A-T-R-I-U-M, a tank stored rainwater. The shrine where the household gods were worshipped .... in the corner of the atrium.

Two small rooms, alae, spelled A-L-A-E, or ...., separated the outer from the inner part of the house. The main room, the tablinum, T-A-B-L-I-N-U-M, ... atrium or hall.

68

The tablinum originally functioned as the reception and dining room, and often as the main bedroom too. Larger houses, however, also had separate dining rooms. The triclinium, dining room, that's T-R-I-C-L-I-N-I-U-M, was generally small, however, too small . . . . family eating or very small-scale entertainment. Finally, at the far end of the house, could be found the peristyle — P-E-R-I-S-T-Y-L-U-M — peristylum in Latin, ..., frequently colonnaded that is, with a row, or rows, of columns around it. Bedrooms were to be found in different parts of the house. . . . . the atrium.

8. Controlled note-making

Now listen to Part 2 of the talk, and complete the notes. Each space is for one word, abbreviation or symbol.

Ho. on . . . . axis

Layout

1. . . . . corner = ... gdn
2. . . . . + ... corners = shops
3. Main dr → a) . . . .
              b) . . . .
4. Bedrms
      a) 2 each side of . . . .
      b) inner, front of . . . ., approx. = dimens.
5. Tablinum
      a) opens on . . . .
      b) flanked . . . .,
         lgr on . . . .

9. Labelling

Listen to Part 2 of the talk again. As you do, use your notes, glossary and the key below to label as many of the different parts of the House of the Surgeon as possible. Note that one of the items in the key cannot be identified from the talk.

Key
M   Main door
B   Bedroom
C   Corridor
D   Dining Room
G   Garden
H   Hall
R   Main Room
S   Shop
W   Wing

House of the Surgeon, Pompeii

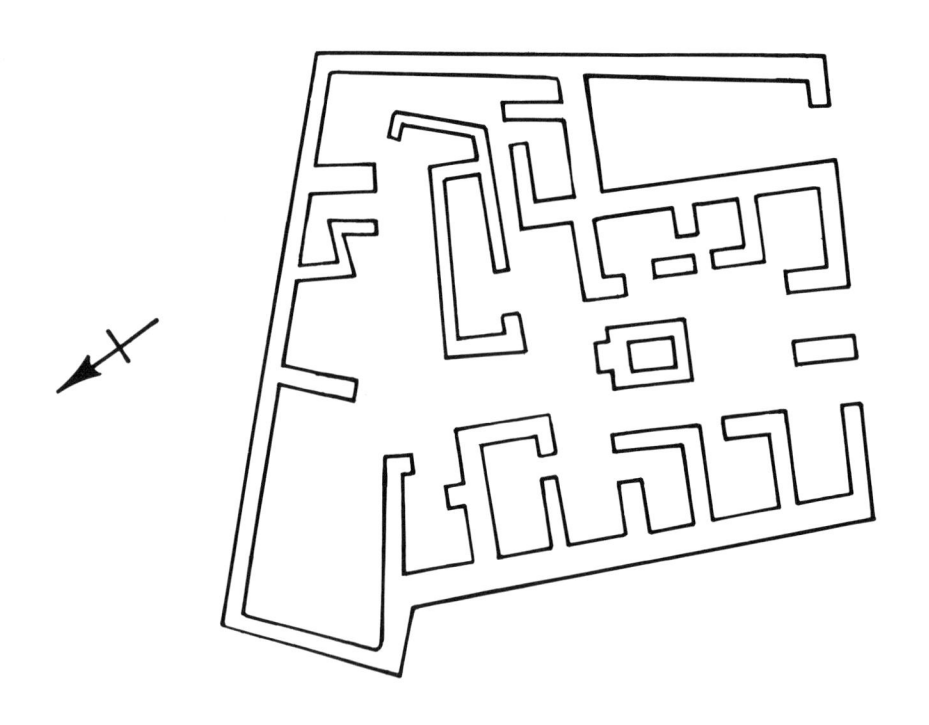

Unit 13 Lasers and Holograms

Reading

Pre-read
1. Think of three facts related to light.
2. Do you know what a laser is? Try to define it.
3. Name some of the uses to which lasers are put.
4. What is a 3-D photograph?
5. A hologram is like a very sophisticated 3-D photograph. Do you know in what way?

Text

Para 1
1 The laser is one example among many of science and technology following art. Many an early writer of science fiction and fantasy visualised the transformation of light into a ray powerful enough to destroy solid material and to cause death to living organisms. In 1960 the development of the first laser
5 translated some of their imaginings into reality.

P2
1 The acronym denotes Light Amplification by Stimulation of Emission of Radiation. Lasers are based on a simple principle of atomic behaviour. Atoms have different levels of energy; those at low levels can be stimulated to higher, for a short time, by the application of heat or light. As they subside from the
5 high energy peak, they will emit light spontaneously.

P3
1 Normally the light thus emitted consists of a whole range of random wavelengths producing incoherent light. However, if the atoms are stimulated by light of a certain wavelength, radiation is produced which is in phase; that is to say, the wavelengths match, crest to crest and trough to trough. In a laser,
5 this resonance results in the amplification of the stimulating input wave. The apparatus produces a powerful output of light in which the speed of emission is many times that of the spontaneously emitted light. Laser light is almost monochromatic due to the resonance process being strongest at the middle of the range of the spontaneously emitted wavelengths.

P4
1 Fig. 1 shows a simplified parallel plate laser. Two end plates, one reflecting, the other only partially so, are positioned at a distance many times their diameter, at either end of the laser medium. As light is directed on to this, the atoms are excited and emit light spontaneously. A wave beginning near an
5 end plate travels through the excited atoms, and begins to rebound between the end plates, moving along a straight axis. (A shutter prevents the wave from escaping through the partially reflecting plate.) The wave thus develops a strong oscillation while it remains in the laser. With the removal of the shutter, part of the wave leaves the apparatus through the partially reflect-
10 ing end plate in the form of a laser beam. This beam travels almost along its axis, emerging, in other words, as a virtually plane wave.
Lasers are generally categorised by the medium in which the excitation takes place. Three basic types are:

Optically pumped solid lasers.   The medium is typically a rod of rare-earth material such as neodymium, or a transition metal such as chromium dispersed in crystal. The optical pump is a powerful light, higher in frequency than the laser light produced. Typically, the laser beam is transmitted in a series of pulsing flashes. This type of laser is less efficient than others, because of the wear and tear caused by the great heat produced in the rod and by the optical pump.

71

Liquid lasers. These lasers are similar to the solid optically pumped, but with a medium consisting of a transparent cylindrical cell containing a liquid such as chloride in selenium oxychloride. Liquid lasers are used to produce pulsed or continuous beams. Their advantage over the solid type is that there are no problems of wear. However, only a few inorganic liquids can be utilised in their construction.

Dye lasers. A dye laser requires another laser to produce excitation in a dye such as rhodamine 6G. The organic dyes produce varied wavelength outputs and can, therefore, be tuned to produce light at different wavelengths in a continuous beam.

Lasers have numerous applications; in construction and precision engineering, for military and medical purposes, and, as we shall hear in the lecture to follow, in holography, or three-dimensional photography.

Fig. 1

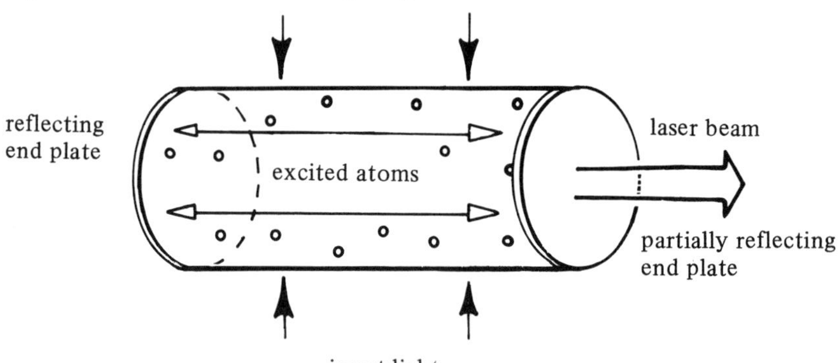

[Diagram of a laser showing: input light entering from top and bottom, reflecting end plate on the left, excited atoms inside the cylinder, partially reflecting end plate on the right, and laser beam exiting to the right.]

1. Content skim

Read the part of the text indicated *as quickly as possible*, and answer.
1. P1 What are the most powerful lasers capable of doing?
2. P2 What may excited atoms do as they subside to a lower level of energy?
3. P3 What terms describe the radiation of: a) natural light? b) laser light?
4. P3/4 Give another two features of laser light.
5. P5 How are lasers categorised?
6. P5 Name three types of laser.

2. Comprehension scan

Read each statement below and decide, *strictly on the basis of the text*, if it is true (T), false (F), or whether there is insufficient evidence (IE) to decide.
1. An acronym is a word composed of the first letters of the words in a phrase.
2. The first laser was powerful enough to destroy solid material and kill living organisms.
3. All types of atom can be used to produce laser light.
4. Natural light is made up of wavelengths which are out of phase.
5. The whole of the light wave within the laser is transmitted in the beam.
6. A plane wave is a light wave travelling along the axis of that wave.
7. Laser light is almost pure white light.
8. Dye lasers are not of the parallel plate type.
9. Lasers can produce either pulsed or continuous beams, but not both.
10. Rhodamine 6G is a transition metal.

3. Guided note-making Read the description in the text of the different types of laser again, and complete the table below.

laser type	material	beam type	partic. advants	disadvants
optically pumped solid	a) e.g. b) e.g.			
liquid	a) e.g.			
dye	a) e.g.			

4. Comparing and contrasting Look at the table below. First, compare the three types of laser; when there is a feature in common write in the appropriate letter in the 'like' section. Then, contrast them; when there is a difference, put the appropriate letter in the 'unlike' column. The first has been done for you.

	optically pumped solid	liquid	dye

optically pumped solid	A. uses solid rod
	 B. prod. puls. beam
	 C. rel. ineffic.
		like │ unlike
		     │ A
		 B │ B
		     │ C
			like │ unlike
			     │ A
			     │ B
			     │ C

liquid	like │ unlike	A. liquid cell B. puls./cont. beam C. no wear + tear	like │ unlike
dye	like │ unlike	like │ unlike	A. liqu. cell B. cont. beam C. diff. wavels

73

5. Writing Now write a paragraph comparing and contrasting the three types of laser according to:
  a) medium
  b) beam type
  c) advantages and disadvantages.

Use your analysis in Exercise 3. Begin: A solid rod is used as the medium in the optically pumped solid laser, in contrast to the other two types, for both liquid and dye lasers have a liquid medium.

Listening

6. Decoding As you listen to Part 1 of the talk, complete the text below.

Holography, the production of three-dimensional ....

................................., is the result of one application of the laser. In face, Dennis Gabor, the inventor of holography, first ....

.... in 1948 as a way of improving the electron microscope. Various difficulties rendered this idea ....,

however, until the development of the laser. Gabor was awarded the Nobel Prize for Physics twenty-three years after ....

.... of the possibilities of the hologram.

A hologram (Gabor's coinage) is a 'total recording' of the optical information ....

The image of an object is recorded on a medium such as a photographic plate or transparency by the use of laser light, and the image of an apparently real object ....

when a laser beam is played upon the 'exposed' recording medium. Let's take a look in ....

at the processes involved in the making of a hologram, and the creation of a holographic image.

7. Labelling Listen to Part 2 of the talk and label the diagram below, marking the laser 'L', the mirror 'M', and the recording medium 'RM'. Then listen to part 3 and place arrows on the lines which represent the light waves to indicate their direction of travel. The object 'O' has already been marked.

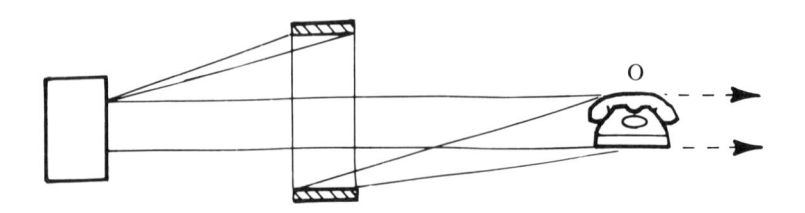

8. Defining Listen carefully to Part 3 of the talk again and note the definitions of the terms below.

interference fringes =

amplitude =

phase information =

coherent light =

9. Controlled note-making Memorise the abbreviations and use them in the notes.
L = laser
O = object
M = mirror
RM = recording medium
IF = interference fringes
ampl. = amplitude
ph. = phase

Now listen to Part 3 of the talk again, and complete the notes. Each space is for one word, abbreviation or symbol.

Making a Holog.

1. .... light direct. on .... + diffract. → RM

2. simul. pt. .... div. +

   .... as

   ....

3. 2 beams   .... → IF i.e.

   a) patt. .... + ... shapes

   b) record of:

   i. .... info. i.e.

   .... in wave ....

   ii. phase info. i.e. ....

   ....

4. waves out of .... = ... → .... image

   " in .... = ... → light ....

75

10. Producing a diagram

Finally, listen to Part 4 of the talk. As you listen, identify each part of the diagram below and label it, using your own abbreviations. Last of all, provide an explanatory key.

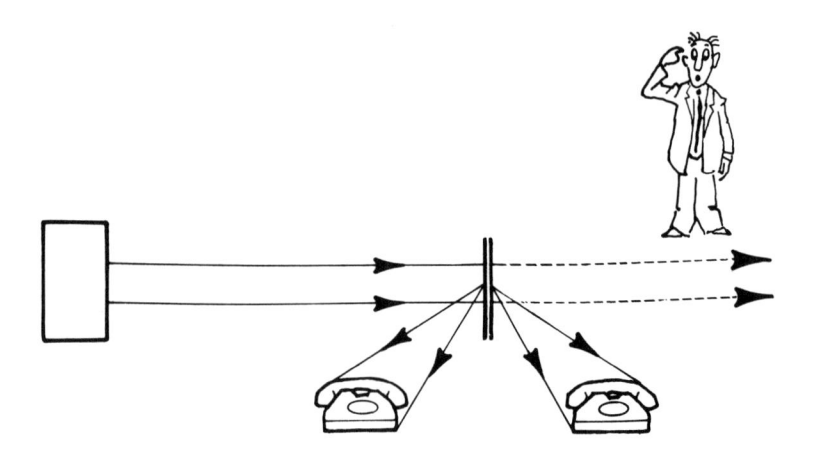

Key

=	=
=	=
=	=

76

Unit 14 Sleep and Dreams

Reading

Pre-read
1. What differences are there in the way the following sleep: a baby; a very old person; you?
2. If you have ever watched the face of a sleeping person closely, what have you observed?
3. Do you know of any explanation for what you saw?
4. How often do you dream?
5. What sort of things do you dream about?
6. Do you believe that it is possible to see into the future in dreams? Why?

Text

> 'Oh sleep! It is a gentle thing,
> Beloved from pole to pole.'

Para 1 1 So wrote Coleridge, and there are few who would disagree with the poet's sentiment. About one-third of your life is spent in this 'gentle' activity, so that by the time you are sixty you will have spent some twenty years of your life asleep.

P2 1 Since evolution has apparently dictated that so much of our time is taken up by sleep, it seems logical to assume that it is of considerable importance to mind and body. Yet science has only just begun to postulate reasons for our need for sleep which are based on research. Scientists, indeed, have even
5 found it difficult to arrive at a satisfactory definition of this daily activity.

P3 1 Some clues may be found, however, when we consider how we sleep, and what happens during sleep. First, its duration and frequency in the day. The average adult sleeps for 7½ hours, while the elderly require one and a half hours less than that. A newborn child, on the other hand, spends two-thirds
5 of the day in sleep. There is a difference, too, in the frequency of sleep during the day. Most children and adults sleep in a single, uninterrupted period. The infant's sleep, by contrast, is polyphasic: that is to say, it occurs at different periods in the twenty-four hours. With the onset of old age, there is a return to the pattern of early childhood. The very old may sleep for only a
10 very limited period during the night, but take naps during the daytime. There is, of course, little in these observations that will be new even to the layman, but when they are linked to what we are beginning to learn about what happens during sleep, it suggests that one important mental function of sleeping is dreaming, and furthermore, that dreaming is of great importance
15 to the very young, who do a great deal of it, but less essential to the aged, who dream much less.

P4 1 What does happen during sleep? For the first sixty to seventy minutes the sleeper's pulse and breathing rates are calm and regular. The electrical activity of the brain is similarly quiet; for most of this period only theta and delta waves, 4 – 7 hertz (cycles per second) and 1 – 2 hertz respectively, occur.
5 The eyes do not move, and there is a slight muscular tension, especially in the region of the throat. When sleepers are awakened from this form of sleep, which is known as orthodox, or NREM, sleep, it is unusual for them to report that they have been dreaming. When they do, it is to describe their dreams as

77

P5 1 having been of a non-visual, thought-like nature.
Then, after the first hour of sleep or so, a new stage is entered for five to fifteen minutes, which is quite different to what has gone before. In contrast to orthodox sleep, the pulse and breathing quicken and become irregular. The EEG waves of the brain speed up to the alpha (8 − 12 hertz), and beta
5 (13 − 22 hertz), levels. This is REM, or rapid eye movement sleep, so called because during it the eyes move rapidly, upwards and downwards, and from side to side. There is also a relaxation of muscular tension. A high proportion of subjects awakened during REM sleep report dreams of a highly visual nature.

P6 1 After this burst of REM activity the sleeper enters another NREM phase. This alternation continues throughout the night, with the NREM phases shortening in contrast to the REM. By the time that the average healthy adult wakes up in the morning, 25% of sleep will have been of the REM type.

P7 1 Sleep, then, probably has a variety of functions, an important one of which is dreaming. This will be considered further in the talk to follow.

1. Content skim

Read the part of the text indicated *as quickly as possible*, and answer.
1. P2 Why does it seem logical to assume that sleep is important?
2. P3 What similarity is there is the sleep patterns of the very young and the very old?
3. P3 What difference is there in the importance of dreaming to the very young and the very old?
4. P4 By what other name is orthodox sleep known?
5. P5 What does REM stand for?

2. Comprehension scan

Read each statement below and decide, *strictly on the basis of the text*, if it is true (T), false (F), or whether there is insufficient evidence (IE) to decide.
1. Coleridge wrote sentimental poetry.
2. A newborn child sleeps for 16 hours a day.
3. 'Polyphasic' means 'in many phases'.
4. The elderly dream less than younger adults because their sleep is polyphasic.
5. The very old, like children, sleep for 16 hours a day.
6. Theta waves travel at 1 − 2 hertz.
7. NREM probably means 'non-rapid eye movement'.
8. During NREM sleep only delta and theta waves are observed.
9. There are four REM and four NREM phases of sleep.
10. REM sleep is caused by irregularity in the pulse rate.

3. Guided note-making

Read P4 and P5 again and complete the frame on this page and on the opposite page by making notes. Two notes have been made for you.

	REM sleep	NREM sleep
1st phase lngth	5 − 15 mins.	
pulse + breath.		calm + reg.
EEG		

	REM sleep	NREM sleep
eye move.		
musc. tens.		
dream.		

4. Writing

Look at the notes above, and then at these sentences which contrast the length of time spent in REM sleep with that spent in NREM sleep.

initial marker *While* ...	*While* the first phase of REM sleep takes 5 – 15 minutes, the first phase of NREM lasts between 60 and 70.
middle markers ... *but* ...	The first phase of REM sleep takes 5 – 15 minutes *but* that of NREM sleep lasts for between 60 and 70.
... *however*, ...	The first phase of REM sleep takes 5 – 15 minutes; *however*, that of NREM sleep lasts 60 – 70.
final marker ... *however*.	The first phase of REM sleep takes 5 – 15 minutes; that of NREM sleep lasts for between 60 and 70, *however*.

Now write five sentences, based upon your notes, contrasting REM with NREM sleep. Use the marker given. Think first about whether the marker would be best at the beginning, in the middle or at the end of the sentence.

1. pulse and breathing (but)
2. EEG (however,)
3. eye movement (While)
4. muscle tension (however,)
5. dream (but)

Listening

5. Decoding

As you listen to Part 1 of the talk, complete the text below.

....
every one of you in this lecture hall what you dreamed about last night, I know the sort ....
.... I would get. ....
.... say they had not dreamed of anything, adding, perhaps, that they never dream. ....
.... rather ordinary and unexciting dreams: the common dream, for example, of re-experiencing ....
.... of the previous day. Some of

79

you would report strange and colourful dreams, of bizarre happenings .... sequences; a type of dream which seems naturally to demand an examination and interpretation .... Others among you, when asked to describe last night's dreams, would blush and refuse to say!

6. Controlled note-making

Listen to Part 2 of the talk and complete the notes. Each space is for one word, abbreviation or symbol.

Dream Functions

1. exper. monit.
   a) mind learns from exper. ....
      .... expers
   b) dream occ. = diff. .... from .... evt.
   e.g. interview dream
2. creat.
   a) helps .... probs. .... suggest. ans./predict. diffs + ...
   b) imag. = ... + product., e.g. .... of 'Dr Jekyll + Mr. Hyde'
   e.g. interview dream .... interv.
3. wish fulfil.
   a) acc. to Freud dreams → satisfact. desires usu. den. by .... / .... / .... of soc.
   e.g. money dream
4. alert. to ext. real.
   a) usu. .... phys. stim.
   e.g. .... dream ← cigarette
5. predict.
   a) comm. .... through ....
   e.g. Joseph's interp. ....

7. Classifying and note-making

Listen to Part 3 of the talk. Decide of which function in the table each dream is an example, and put the letter of the dream against the appropriate function. Then, make a brief note of the dream's content. The first, Dream A, has been classified for you. Note that there is one dream function which is not illustrated by an example.

Function	Dream
experience-monitoring	
creative	
wish-fulfilment	
external reality	A. v. cold – in Finland – quilt fallen from bed
predictive	

8. Writing

a) Dictation
Listen to the description of Dream A in the third part of the talk again. As the cassette is stopped at the end of each phrase, write it down. When the description has ended, read what you have written, and punctuate the text.
Do the same for Dreams B and C, then check your dictations against the transcript of the lecture.
Below are some of the words in the descriptions that you may not be familiar with. Look them up in your dictionary and check their pronunciation.

Dream A	Dream B	Dream C
frozen	bass	gravely
bitterly	audience	telegram
cupped	spell-bound	announcing
awoke	croak	
quilt		

b) Free Writing
Describe a dream which you had recently, or one which has been told to you, or one famous in history.

Unit 15   The World's Weather

Reading

Pre-read
1. What shape is the earth?
2. What imaginary lines divide it: a) vertically from pole to pole?
                                    b) horizontally?
3. Why is Greenwich in London important geographically?
4. How would you adjust your watch when flying east from Greenwich?
5. And if you were flying westward from Greenwich?
6. What other imaginary lines are used in the division of the surface of the earth into zones?

Text 1

Para 1 1 In a conventional atlas the earth is depicted as a spheroid with a horizontal line around its middle. This is the equator, which divides the earth into northern and southern hemispheres, and which is calculated as the 0° (zero degrees) line of latitude. The North Pole is situated at the 'top' of the
        5 northern hemisphere, with the arctic regions extending southwards to the Arctic Circle at 66°33′N (sixty-six degrees, thirty-three minutes North) of the equator.

P2   1 The belt of the tropics stretches northwards from the equator to latitude 23° 28′N, the boundary line of the Tropic of Cancer. Between the tropics and the Arctic Circle lie the temperate zones, so-called in basic geography because the climate of these regions does not reach the extremes of heat and cold of
        5 the tropical and Arctic regions.

P3   1 The southern hemisphere displays imaginary lines of division at the same points as the northern, but with the tropic being that of Capricorn, and the southernmost, Antarctic, region stretching from the South Pole to the Antarctic Circle.

P4   1 The weather of the world, however, does not fit neatly into the spaces between these lines in either hemisphere. For example, in summer in the northern hemisphere, the tropical monsoon belt extends to 30°N in southern Asia, but reaches no farther than 20°N in West Africa. Climatology and
        5 meteorology, the sciences of climate and weather, therefore, use a basic division of the earth into low, mid and high latitude zones; the low latitudes lie between the Equator and 30°N and S, while the mid and high latitude zones are divided at 60°.

1. Content skim

Read the part of the text indicated *as quickly as possible*, and answer.
1. P1 What is being described?
2. P2 Which hemisphere is the tropic of Cancer in?
      How many zones are described? What are they?
3. P3 What are the similarities between the hemispheres?
      What are the differences in name?
4. P4 How many zones do climatologists divide the world into?
      Name them.

2. Labelling

Read P1 – 3 again and
a) label the Equator, Tropics of Cancer and Capricorn, the North and South Poles, and the Arctic and Antarctic Circles.
b) mark in their degrees of latitude.

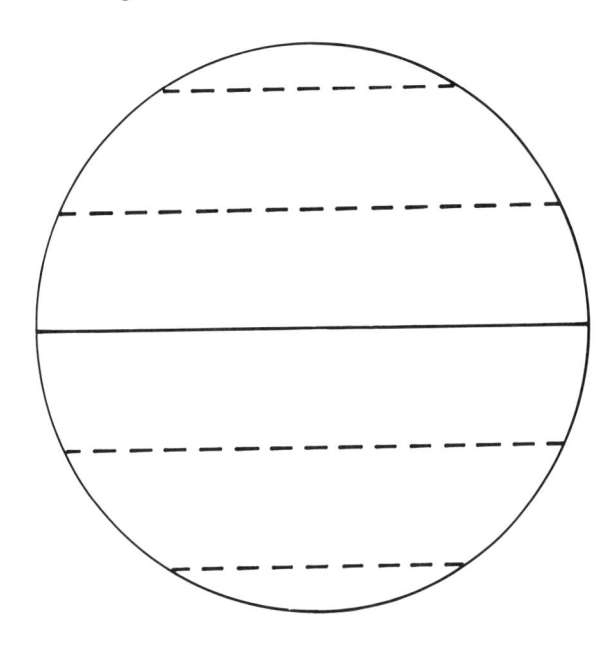

3. Labelling

Read P4 again and
a) mark the Equator, and 30° and 60° lines of latitude north and south.
b) label the high, low and mid-latitude zones.

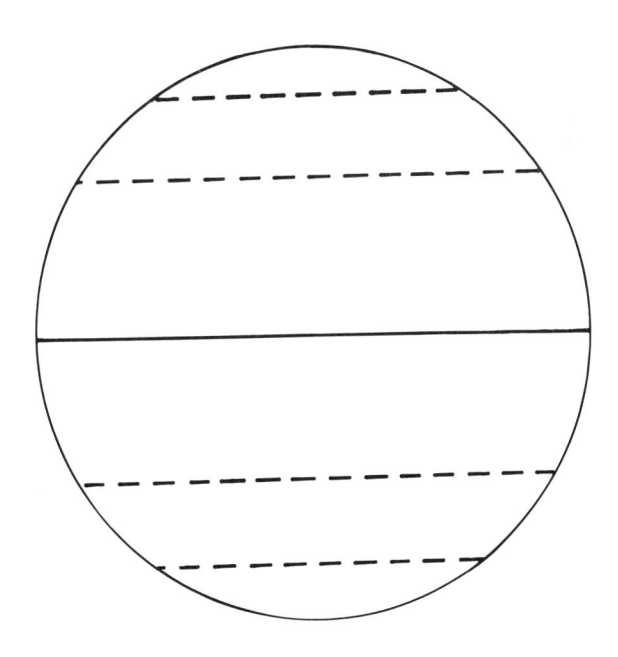

83

Text 2

Para 1 1 Climatology and meteorology must take into account not only the division of the surface of the earth into zones, but also its atmosphere. The envelope of gases which surrounds the earth is divided into layers differentiated by temperature change, and certain other features such as water content. The lower
5 atmosphere is composed of the troposphere and stratosphere, while the mesosphere constitutes the first layer of the upper.

P2 1 The troposphere is that part of the atmosphere in which we live and in which weather phenomena are most marked. The troposphere is not uniform in height around the earth. The heat of the sun and its related convective disturbances at the equator produce a troposphere 16 km high; above the poles,
5 however, it extends to only half that height. The troposphere contains 75 − 80% of the atmosphere's mass of gases and water vapour. Temperatures decrease with height in this part of the atmosphere, at a mean rate of $6.5°C$ per kilometre, up to the tropopause, the boundary between the troposphere and the layer of increasing temperatures above it, the stratosphere.

P3 1 This layer reaches up from the tropopause to the next point of temperature inversion, the stratopause, at a height of 50 km. The stratosphere contains most of the ozone in the atmosphere, and it is its absorption of the sun's ultraviolet radiation, combined with the lower air density, which causes
5 temperatures in the stratosphere to increase with height. At the stratopause, in fact, temperatures are similar to those at sea level. The temperature inversion between tropopause and stratopause means that the troposphere is largely self-contained, as convection from its lower temperature higher regions is inhibited by the ceiling of increasing temperatures above it.

P4 1 The upper atmosphere begins at the stratopause with another reversal in the temperature trend. The mesosphere extends for 30 km above the stratopause, and temperatures behave as in the troposphere, although at a different rate of change.

P5 1 With height, too, present-day knowledge of the workings of the atmosphere diminishes, but for the purpose of creating a simple model of aspects of the earth's climate, this description of the first three layers of the atmosphere should be sufficient.

4. Comprehension scan

Read each statement below and decide, *strictly on the basis of the text*, if it is true (T), false (F), or whether there is insufficient evidence (IE) to decide.
1. The atmosphere is defined as an envelope of gases.
2. The atmosphere is divided into three parts.
3. The troposphere is half a kilometre high above the poles.
4. Weather phenomena are most marked in the troposphere because of its water content.
5. The temperature range in the stratosphere is similar to that in the troposphere.
6. When the temperature at sea level is $19.5°C$, the temperature 3 km overhead is always $0°C$.
7. The stratosphere is uniform in depth.
8. The mesopause occurs at a height of 80 km.
9. Temperatures decrease with height in the mesosphere.
10. The stratosphere contains 20 − 25% of the atmosphere's mass of gases and water vapour.

5. Controlled note-making

Read Text 2 again, and complete these notes. Each space is for one word.

The Earth's Atmosphere

A	lwr. atmos.	1. tropos.
		a) ht. @ equat. = ...
		← heat sun + ...
T		ht. @ poles = ...
		b) cont. = 75 − 80% ....
M		gases + H_2O ....
		c) temps. ↓ with .... 6.5°C
O		.... on av.
		d) tropop. = bound. − temps. ....
S		e) convect. inhib. stratos. ....
		.... ∴ tropos. lgly
P		.... − ....
		2. stratos.
H		a) ht. = tropop. − ....
		b) cont. .... of ozone in ....
E		c) temps. ↑ ← ozone absorpt.
		sun's .... +
R		lwr. ....
	upp. atmos.	3. mesos.
E		a) ht. = stratop. − ....
		b) temps. ....

85

6. Transferring information

Read the notes you made on p85 and:
a) shade in the troposphere: |||
           the stratosphere: ≡
           the mesosphere: ///
b) identify, with heights, the tropopause by a T
                      the stratopause " " S
                      the mesopause " " M
c) mark zones of falling temperatures ↓ and zones of rising temperatures ↑

Listening

7. Decoding

As you listen to Parts 1 and 2 of the talk, complete the text below.

We are going to proceed from our brief consideration of the earth's

.... to look at one of the basic factors in the planet's weather, the ....

.... wind system.

To reduce a complex system ....

.... proportions, the general direction of the wind flows

over the surface of the earth ....

.... as follows; it is, of course, important to remember

that when we talk of a wind we name it by that part ....

.... from which it blows. That is

to say, a west wind is one blowing ....

.... towards the east.

On a planetary scale, then, the ....
.... winds in the mid-latitudes of both ....
.... are the westerlies. In
.... on
either side of the equator they ....
.... – from the east – and traditionally known as the
'Trades', the name given to them ....
.... The Trades of the northern hemisphere blow
from the north-east, their ....
.... on the other side of the line, from the south-east. In
the high latitudes, although ....
.... as in the others, the prevailing winds are generally
held to be from the east, and are named the 'Polar Easterlies'.

8. Transferring information

Read the completed transcript in 7 again, and complete the diagram of the planetary wind system, using the key.

Key

Symbol	Direction	Name
⇙⇙	NE	North-east Trades
⇖⇖	SE	South-east Trades
→	W	Westerlies
⇠----	E	Polar Easterlies

87

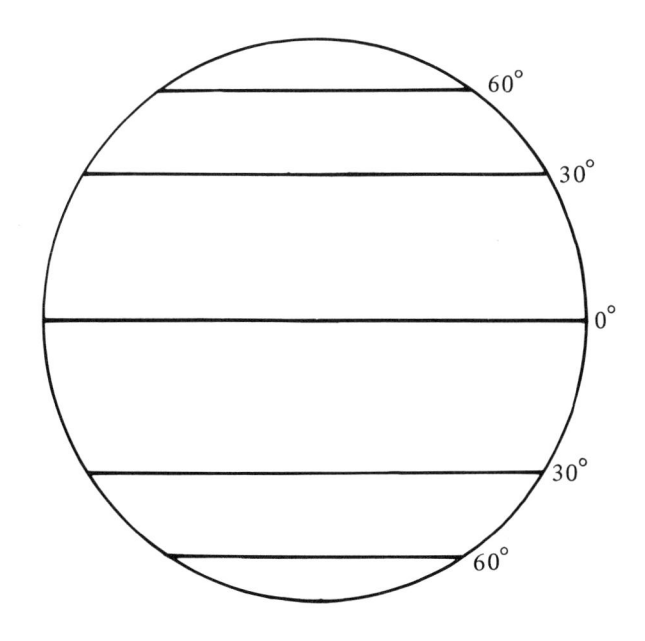

9. Abbreviating

Listen to Part 3 of the talk. Then complete the key below by devising a suitable abbreviation for each item. The first one has been done for you.

Key

PTP... Polar Tropopause   ...... Mid-latitude Westerlies

...... Tropical Tropopause   ...... Polar Night Jet Stream

...... Stratopause   ...... Mesopheric Easterlies

...... Tropical Easterlies   ...... Mesopheric Westerlies

...... Inter-tropical Convergence ...... Jet Stream
       Zone

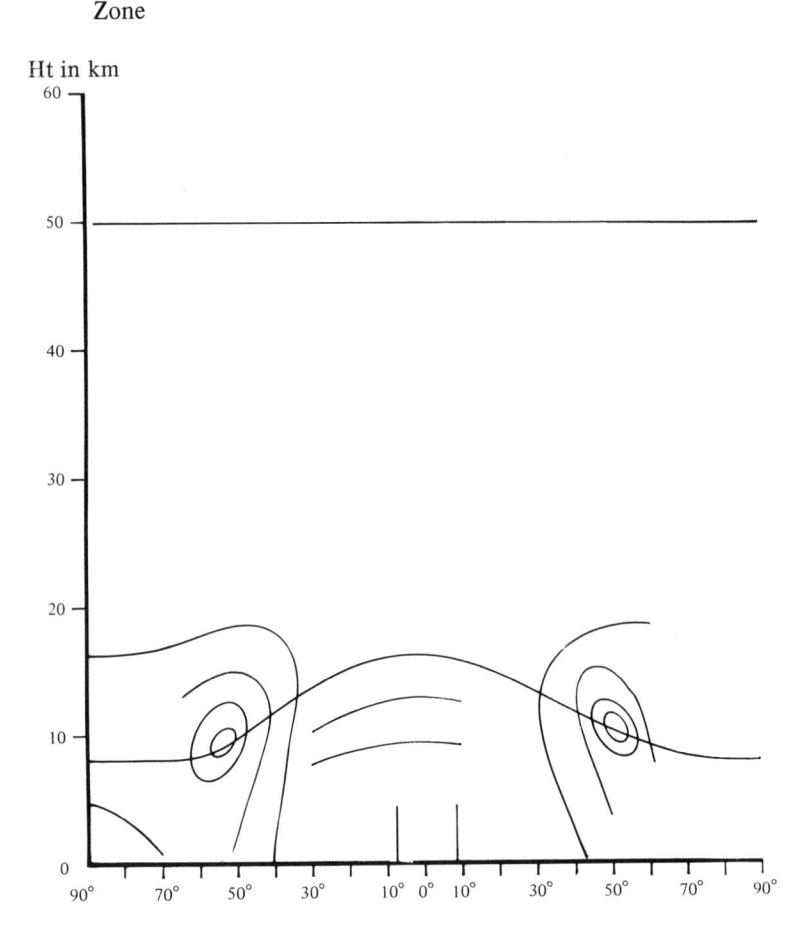

Ht in km

10. Labelling

Listen to Part 3 of the talk again and label the diagram above using your abbreviations from the key. Note that some items in the talk do not appear on the diagram, and some features on the diagram are not mentioned in the talk.

Unit 16   Heat Control & The Skin

Listening

1. Note-making

You will hear a talk in three parts:
Part I   How the body gains and loses heat.
Part II   "   "   "   "   "   "   "
Part III   What happens in cases of fever.
As you listen, make full notes.

2. Note-making

List ways in which the body
a) gains heat.
b) loses heat.

3. Sequencing

The area of the brain which acts as the body's thermostat is called the hypothalamus. Draw two flowcharts to show
a) what happens when the body needs to conserve heat.
b) what happens when the body needs to lose heat.

4. Writing

Write a short paragraph explaining the mechanism which produces fever in some infections. You may illustrate your explanation.

5. Explaining

Explain in note form how the following kinds of behaviour help keep the people concerned warm and cool respectively.
a) It was mid winter in England, and Helen's central heating had broken down. She went to the bedroom and put on an extra sweater, then she came back into the sitting-room, shut the door and sat down in her softest armchair. She rubbed her hands together and wriggled her toes for a while. Then she realised that the sweater was a bit damp, so she went and changed it for another one.
b) Legwa lives in tropical Africa. He wears very thin, white cotton clothes and in the heat of the day prefers to sit on a stone slab under the window. If he has to work indoors he usually has an electric fan running. He takes a cold shower twice a day.

Reading

Text

The structure of the skin

The skin consists of two main regions:
1. *The epidermis.*   This is the outer layer and consists chiefly of dead, dry, flattened cells which rub off from time to time. More cells are produced from the layer of living cells at the bottom of the epidermis.
2. *The dermis.*   This is the deeper layer and consists of living cells of connective tissue, the lowest layer being of cells which contain stored fat. It has a network of nerves and blood vessels running through it, the nerve endings lying just below the epidermis. The dermis contains the following structures which continue outwards through the epidermis:
a) The sweat glands. These are coiled tubes which open on to the surface of the skin.

b) The hairs and oil glands. The hairs grow from the bottom of deep pits and the oil glands open into these pits.

c) The nails. These grow from roots in the dermis and are like the cells of the epidermis only much more tightly packed together, giving a hard, smooth structure.

The functions of the skin

1. *To provide the sense of touch.* It does this by means of the nerve endings and touch bodies (special type of nerve endings) which lie just below the epidermis. Some of these endings are sensitive to heat, others to cold, pain, etc. The message then passes along the sensory nerve fibres of a lateral nerve from the skin to the spinal cord and so to the brain. These sensitive nerve endings are protected from injury by the dead layer of the epidermis which lies above them.
2. *To protect the body against injury, bruising, etc.* It does this by means of the epidermis, and the hairs. The epidermis is a dead, tough layer and so forms a non-sensitive, protective cover to the dermis and the muscles. The hairs protecting the scalp give extra protection to the brain and, like all the hairs of the body can be made to stand on end by means of muscles attached to their lower ends.
3. *To protect the body against the effects of strong sunshine.* It does this by means of the cells which form a layer at the bottom of the epidermis. If the skin is exposed to bright sunshine these cells produce a dark-coloured substance (this is what happens when we get sunburnt) and this dark substance is able to absorb the sun's heat and so prevent the dermis from being damaged.
4. *To protect the body against infection.* It does this by means of the epidermis and the oil glands. The epidermis is a dry, scaly, dead layer and so microbes (bacteria and other disease-causing organisms) are unable to get through it to the living cells below. The oil produced by the oil glands contains a substance which tends to kill microbes and this oil flows out over the hairs and skin.
5. *To help regulate the body temperature.* It does this by means of sweat glands, blood vessels and fat cells.
6. *To store food.* It does this by means of the fat cells which form a layer at the bottom of the dermis. Many foods which have been eaten, but are not required for immediate use, are changed to droplets of fat and stored in these cells. The fat can be moved back from the cells into the blood and used when and where it is needed.
7. *To produce vitamin D.* This vitamin is produced by the action of sunlight on the fat in the fat cells.
8. *To prevent loss of water from the body.* It does this by means of the epidermis. This is a dry, waterproof layer and hence is able to prevent water evaporating from the living tissues into the air.
9. *To get rid of waste products.* It does this by means of the sweat glands, the sweat produced being mainly water but having some mineral salts dissolved in it. The amount of waste matter removed in this way is extremely small and this is not an important function of the skin.

The blood supply to the skin

There is a large capillary network in the dermis, arterial blood being brought to it by small arteries which branch off from the aorta. Venous blood is removed from it by branch veins leading into the vena cava. The network of capillaries is particularly dense around the coiled part of the sweat glands because these are regions of great activity.

The nerve supply to the skin

Sensory nerve fibres lead from the nerve endings in the dermis to the brain and spinal cord, and action fibres lead from the chain of sympathetic ganglia to the small arteries in the dermis and also to the hair muscles and sweat glands. These action fibres are part of the autonomic system.
(from Hubbard, D. V. 1965: *Your Body/How it Works*)

6. Content skim

Glance over the reading passage and then answer the following questions:
1. How is this passage organised?
2. How many main layers has the skin?
3. In general terms, what is the most comprehensive function of the skin?
Read again the section on *The structure of the skin*.
4. How many layers are found within a) the epidermis and b) the dermis?
5. Which structures are in contact with both the dermis and the epidermis?

7. Comprehension scan

Decide whether each of the following is true or false.
1. The epidermis is made up mainly of living cells.
2. Fat is stored in living cells in the epidermis.
3. At least two kinds of glands are found in the dermis.
4. Different nerve endings in the dermis have different functions.
5. The dead cells of the epidermis are our main protection against sunburn.
6. The cells of the epidermis contain a substance which kills bacteria.
7. The sweat glands and the blood vessels are the two ways the skin has of regulating temperature.
8. Droplets of fat nourish the dermis.
9. The sweat glands have a rich blood supply.
10. Some blood vessels in the dermis are supplied with nerves.

8. Note-making

List the parts played in the functions of the skin by each of the following:
1. The epidermis; 2. Fat cells in the dermis; 3. Glands

9. Identifying

Complete the key to the diagram.

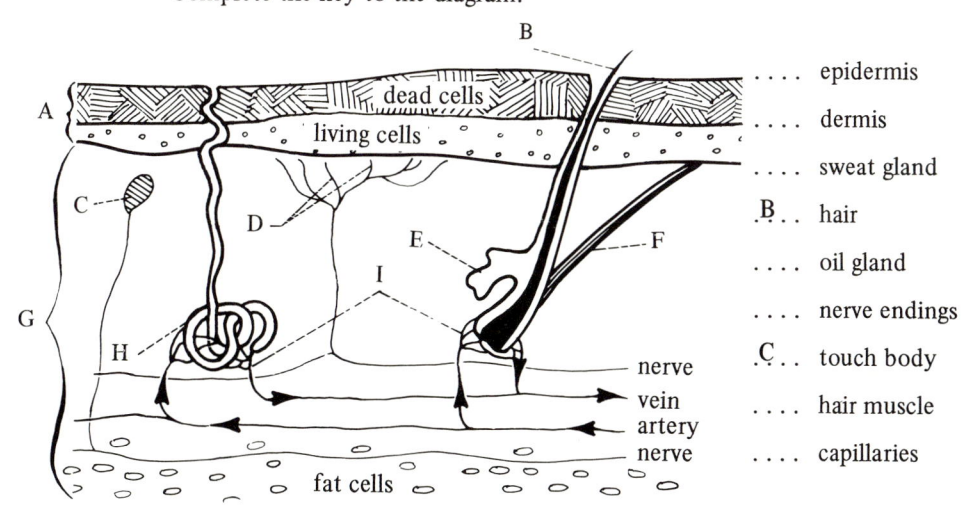

.... epidermis
.... dermis
.... sweat gland
.B.. hair
.... oil gland
.... nerve endings
.C.. touch body
.... hair muscle
.... capillaries

10. Writing

Write a short paragraph explaining simply how the skin prevents undesirable things from happening to us.

Unit 17   Computers

Listening

1. Note-making

Make full notes as you listen to the talk. The main points covered in each part are as follows:
Part 1   Computers: general
                     use in banking
Part 2   Use in medicine
Part 3   Use in newspaper production and as word processors

2. Defining

Complete the following:

A computer is . . .
It differs from previous methods in two important ways:

a)

b)

3. Listing

List four aspects of banking in which computers are being used increasingly.

a)

b)

c)

d)

4. Sequencing

Here is a simple flowchart for boiling an egg. Construct a similar one to show how cheques are processed.

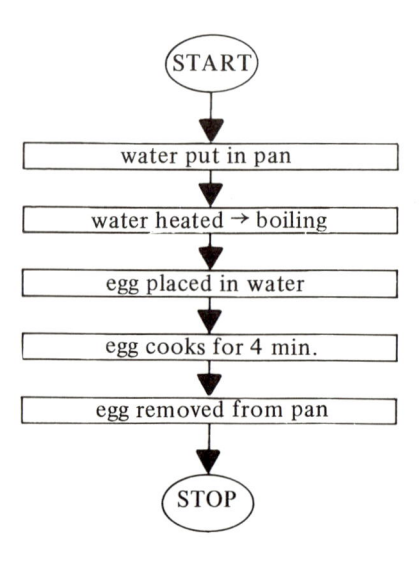

```
         START
           ↓
   water put in pan
           ↓
   water heated → boiling
           ↓
   egg placed in water
           ↓
   egg cooks for 4 min.
           ↓
   egg removed from pan
           ↓
          STOP
```

5. Describing

Complete the following diagram to show where computers are used in hospitals.

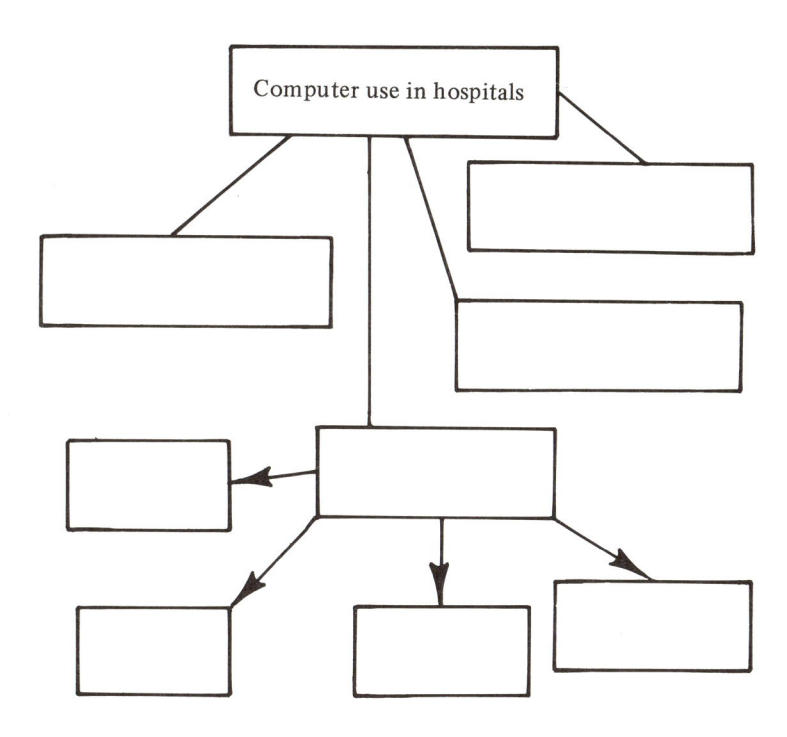

```
                    ┌─────────────────────────┐
                    │ Computer use in hospitals│
                    └─────────────────────────┘
                       /        |        \
              ┌──────────┐      |      ┌──────────────┐
              │          │      |      │              │
              └──────────┘      |      └──────────────┘
                                |      ┌──────────────┐
                                |      │              │
                                |      └──────────────┘
                                |
                    ┌─────────────────────────┐
           ┌────────│                         │────────┐
           ↓        └─────────────────────────┘        ↓
        ┌──────┐           |          |            ┌──────────┐
        │      │           ↓          ↓            │          │
        └──────┘       ┌──────┐   ┌──────┐         └──────────┘
                       │      │   │      │
                       └──────┘   └──────┘
```

6. Sequencing

Construct a diagram to show how computers are used to assist medical diagnosis. Use arrows to show the direction of information flow.

7. Sequencing and comparing

Produce flowcharts for the non-computerised and the computerised systems of newspaper production you heard about. Set them out side by side to illustrate the simplification brought about by the use of computers.
Who are the people whose jobs are most obviously affected by these changes?

8. Writing

Jane was given a piece of typing to do by Mrs Massey, her supervisor. She made several mistakes and had to paint them out and type in the corrections. Then she realised she had missed out a line in the middle of a paragraph, so she had to retype the whole document. Then Mrs Massey came in and asked her to add an extra paragraph in the middle and change the order of two other paragraphs. Jane sighed and got more paper and carbon out of her drawer.
Write a note to Jane, explaining how a word processor would make her work easier for her.

Reading

Text

Para 1   1   Much hostility towards computers has been based on the fear of widespread unemployment resulting from their introduction. One of the earliest examples of this was the burning of Jacquard's punched-card operated looms by the weavers of Lyons*. Computers are often installed as part of automated
         5   production systems requiring a minimum of operators, resulting in the loss of many jobs. This has happened, for example, in many steelworks.

93

P2 1 On the other hand, computers do create jobs. They are more skilled and better paid, though fewer in number than those they replace. Many activities could not continue in their present form without computers, no matter how many people were employed. Examples are the cheque clearing system of
5 major banks, and the weather forecasting system.

P3 1 When a firm introduces computers, a few new people are usually employed in key posts (such as operations manager) while other staff are re-trained as operators, programmers and data preparation staff. After the new system has settled down, people in non-computer jobs are not always replaced when
5 they leave, resulting in a decrease in the number of employees. This decrease is sometimes offset by a substantial increase in the activity of the firm, resulting from the introduction of computers.

P4 1 The attitudes of trade unions towards computers vary. There is fear of widespread unemployment, and of the takeover of many jobs by computer trained workers, making promotion for older workers, not skilled in the use of computers, more difficult. In early 1977, the British Transport and General
5 Workers Union announced its intention to close its own data processing department because 'computers put people out of work'.

P5 1 On the other hand, many trade unionists see the drift towards computers as inevitable. They feel that their contribution to greater efficiency and productivity will improve the condition of the whole economy, and lead to the creation of more jobs. This view was endorsed by the British Prime Minister,
5 James Callaghan, in January 1979, when he made the point that new technologies hold the key to increased productivity, which will benefit the economy in the long run.

P6 1 There has been a recent drive by several trade unions to recruit members from data processing personnel. A significant proportion of computer operators, programmers, systems analysts and data processing managers are trade union members.   (from Bishop, P. 1981: *Comprehensive Computer Studies*)

*An early instance of automatic information processing from the history of computer development. The cards, introduced in c 1802, enabled looms to weave complex patterns automatically.

9. Content skim Read the first sentence of each paragraph. What is the topic of each paragraph?

10. Comprehension scan
P1.3 What does 'this' refer to?
P1.6 What part of the steelworks is referred to?
P2.2 Typically, what kinds of jobs do they replace?
P3.   Which three groups of staff does this paragraph refer to?
P3.7 What results from the introduction of computers?
P4.1 Where are examples given of this variety of attitudes?
P4.6 Why are the words 'computers put people out of work' in inverted commas?
P5.2 Who does 'their' refer to?
P5.3 What will lead to the creation of more jobs?
P5.4 Which view is referred to?
P5.6 What will benefit the economy?
P6.   Which two groups are contrasted in this paragraph?

11. Paragraph analysis — note-making

Study the chart. It shows in diagram form the structure of the passage, paragraph by paragraph. Compare it carefully with the passage and then complete it in note form.

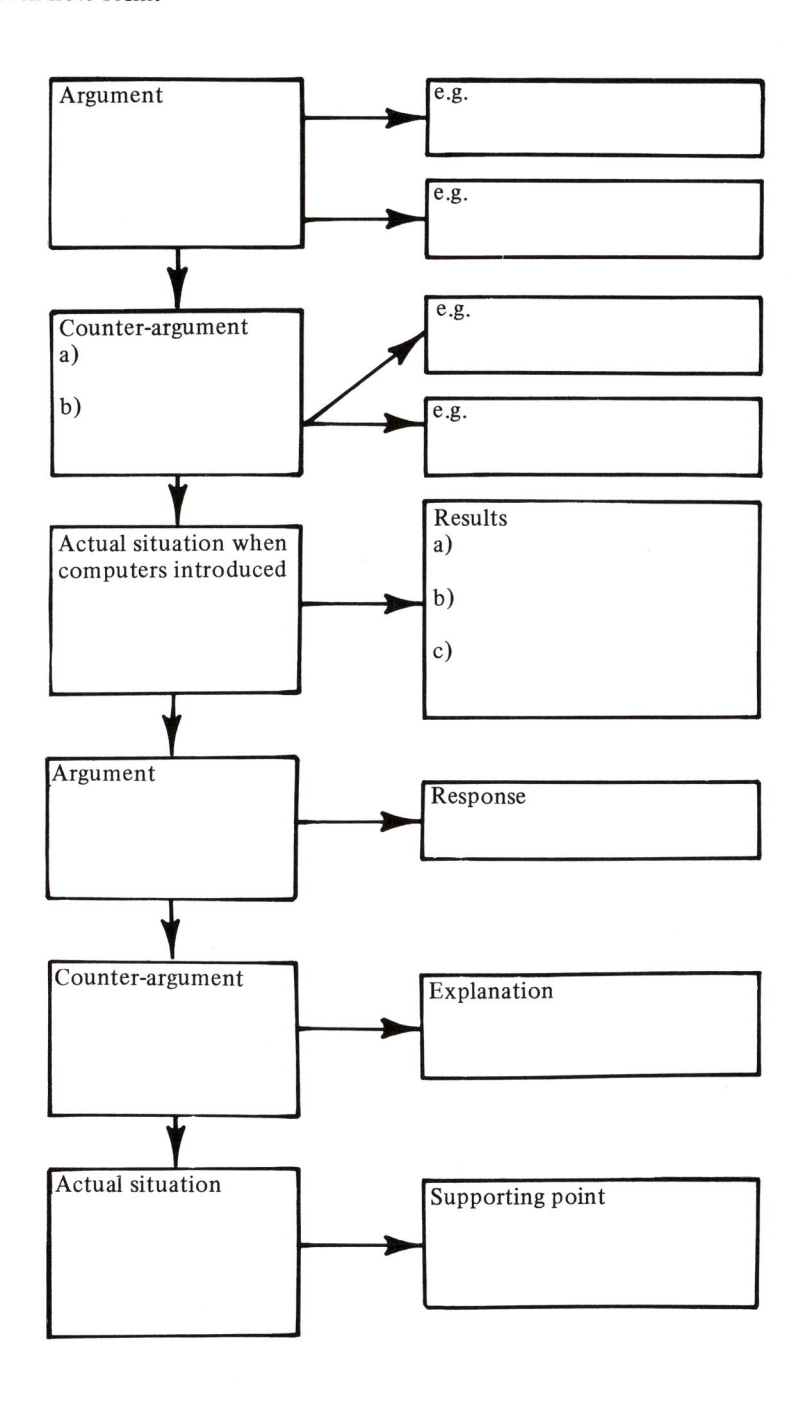

```
┌─────────────────┐      ┌─────────────────────┐
│ Argument        │─────▶│ e.g.                │
│                 │      └─────────────────────┘
│                 │      ┌─────────────────────┐
│                 │─────▶│ e.g.                │
└────────┬────────┘      └─────────────────────┘
         ▼
┌─────────────────┐      ┌─────────────────────┐
│ Counter-argument│─────▶│ e.g.                │
│ a)              │      └─────────────────────┘
│                 │      ┌─────────────────────┐
│ b)              │─────▶│ e.g.                │
└────────┬────────┘      └─────────────────────┘
         ▼
┌─────────────────┐      ┌─────────────────────┐
│ Actual situation│      │ Results             │
│ when computers  │      │ a)                  │
│ introduced      │─────▶│ b)                  │
│                 │      │ c)                  │
└────────┬────────┘      └─────────────────────┘
         ▼
┌─────────────────┐      ┌─────────────────────┐
│ Argument        │─────▶│ Response            │
└────────┬────────┘      └─────────────────────┘
         ▼
┌─────────────────┐      ┌─────────────────────┐
│ Counter-argument│─────▶│ Explanation         │
└────────┬────────┘      └─────────────────────┘
         ▼
┌─────────────────┐      ┌─────────────────────┐
│ Actual situation│─────▶│ Supporting point    │
└─────────────────┘      └─────────────────────┘
```

12. Writing

When you have completed and checked the chart, use it to write *one* paragraph explaining current views on computerisation.

Unit 18 Arthritis

Listening

1. Note-making

You will hear a talk in three parts. Make full notes on each part as you listen.
Part 1   Types of joint in the body
Part 2   Osteoarthritis
    1. Incidence 2. Causes 3. Pathology 4. Symptoms 5. Treatment
Part 3   Rheumatoid arthritis: as for Part 2

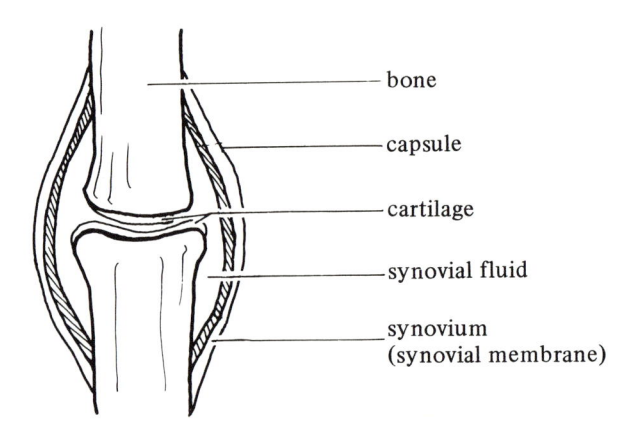

- bone
- capsule
- cartilage
- synovial fluid
- synovium (synovial membrane)

Note: The ends of the joints would normally be in contact but are separated here for clarity.

2. Classifying

Draw a classification diagram of types of joint. Give an example of each type.

3. Note-making

Complete the following chart to summarise the information given about osteo- and rheumatoid arthritis.

	osteoarthritis	rheumatoid arthritis
Incidence		

4. Classifying

Examine these diagrams. Decide in each case whether the diagram shows
a) a case of osteoarthritis   (mark OA)
b) a case of rheumatoid arthritis   (mark RA)
c) neither condition   (mark X)

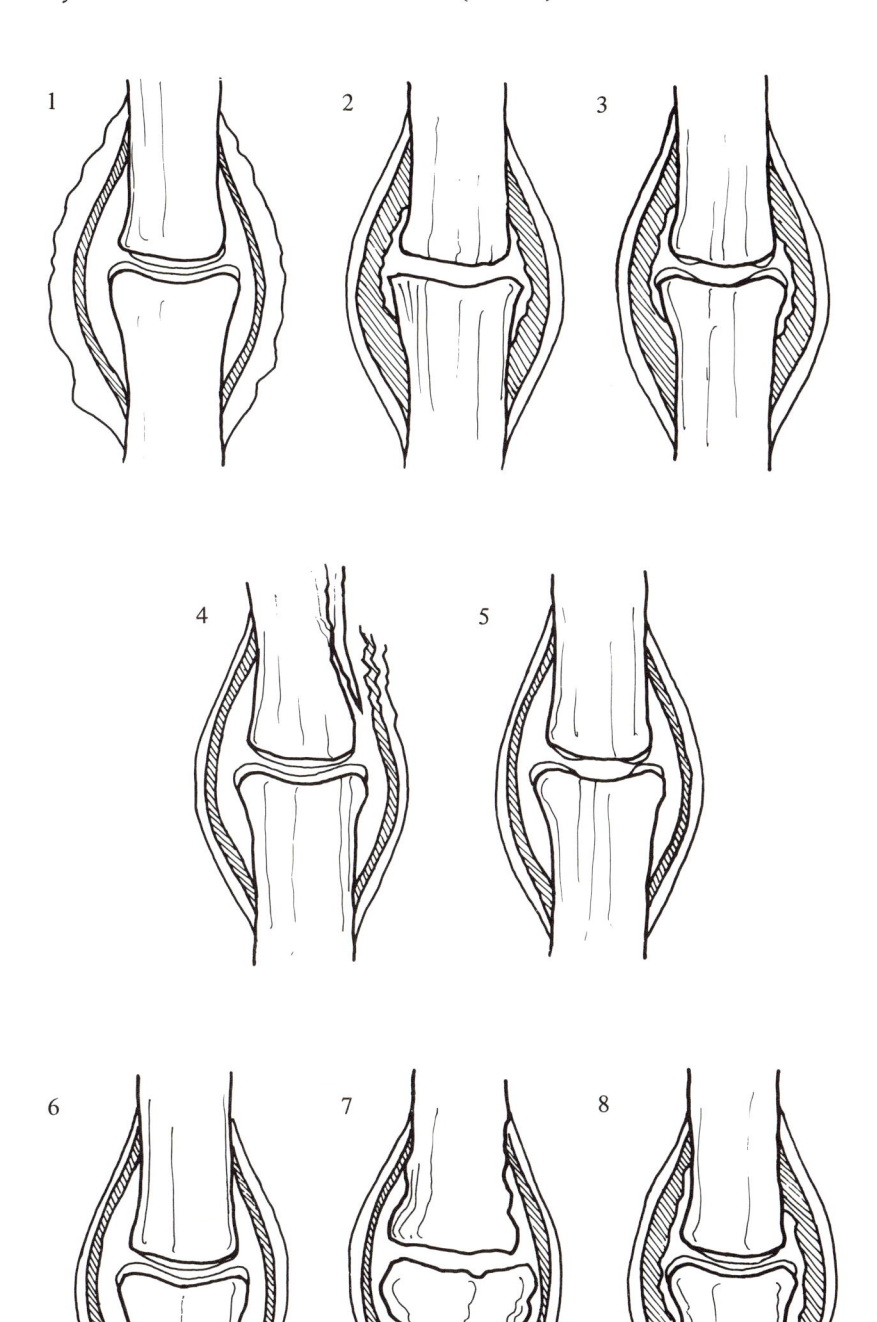

Reading

My Research

Dr. Valerie E. Jones, Royal Devon and Exeter Hospital and University of Exeter.

Para 1   Some event or infection must trigger rheumatoid arthritis (RA) and the ultimate aim of most scientists working in arthritis research is to find this trigger or cause. It is our aim too. But application of highly sophisticated techniques to look directly for the cause have been unsuccessful so far and, after all, research is 'the art of the soluble'. So we have devised a more indirect backdoor approach to the problem and furthermore are looking at the earliest possible stages of the disease.

P2   Working in a rural area like Devon we are well placed and make every effort to see people when they are suffering their earliest arthritic symptoms. This is usually long before they are diagnosed as having rheumatoid arthritis, and indeed many of them do not develop the disease. Also very few of our patients move away from this area so we continue to see them every few months to detect any small changes taking place in the disease process.

P3   When people develop rheumatoid arthritis they usually get a characteristic antibody in their blood and joint fluids called rheumatoid factor. This antibody reacts with a protein called 'altered IgG', also in the arthritic person's body fluids. It is the nature and properties of this 'altered IgG' which we are studying because we think it will give us vital information (albeit indirect) about the cause of rheumatoid arthritis. In other words, if you want to catch a thief, first go out and find a policeman and a detective.

P4   So first we measure the rheumatoid factors (the policemen). These are easily recognised and identified (just as policemen wear uniforms). But policemen come in all shapes and sizes and so do rheumatoid factors. So when they first appear in the blood in the earliest stages of the disease, their size, appearance and other characteristics are measured and documented.

P5   The 'altered IgG' (the detective) is a much more difficult problem. Because detectives are plain clothes policemen they are not easy to identify in a huge crowd of people. Similarly, 'altered IgG' is a minute part of a huge population of IgG molecules which everybody possesses as part of their arsenal for defence against infection and disease.

P6   Therefore there are numerous questions to be answered. Indeed, does 'altered IgG' really exist in rheumatoid patients? There are many indications that it does, but not enough rockhard evidence. Using very sensitive methods we have looked for traces in blood and joint fluids but have found no clearcut differences between RA patients and normal people. We are now looking for ways to isolate this 'altered IgG' from the blood of rheumatoid patients. It should be much more easily characterised once it is free of the huge population of similar but not quite identical normal IgG molecules.

P7   One thing we do find is that rheumatoid factors appear very early on, when people first begin to suffer joint pains, often long before RA can be reliably diagnosed. So the trigger has already provoked the patient's body system into manufacturing 'altered IgG' (the detectives have already been alerted and are searching for the thief and the police are backing them up).

P8   This indicates a need for potential sufferers of RA to be seen and treated very early if the disease progression is to be halted. But before this can happen we need more reliable early diagnostic signs. More information about 'altered IgG' should help us to devise such diagnostic tests as well as help us to catch the thief — the cause of RA.

'altered IgG' cause of RA
(detective)   (thief)

Rheumatoid factor
(policeman)

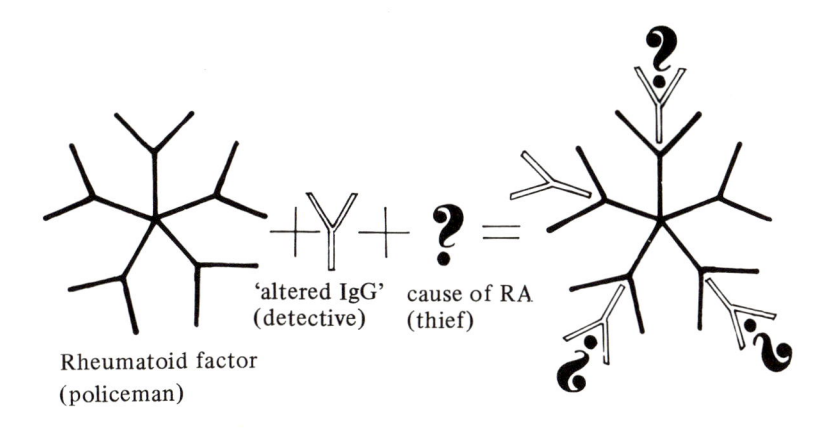

This illustrates Dr. Jones' detective work in looking for the cause of rheumatoid arthritis.

5. Content skim Look quickly through the passage and decide, in general, what it is about.

6. Comprehension scan
- P2.2 What does 'This' refer to
- P2.4 Who is referred to by 'them'?
  'Also' introduces a second point. What was the first one?
- P2.5 Which area is referred to?
- P3.6 What figure of speech is intoduced here by 'in other words'?
- P4.4 The size of what?
- P5. What new metaphor is used in this paragraph?
- P6. What factor in the situation raises these questions?
- P6.4 What is 'traces' a reference to?
- P6. What possible reason is given for the fact that they have 'found no clear-cut differences'?
- P7.1 Why 'do find'?
  What, according to the metaphor, are the rheumatoid factors?
- P8.1 What does 'this' refer to?
- P8.2 What does 'this' refer to?
- P8.5 What is the identity of the 'thief'?

7. Note-making
a) Write down suitable headings for each paragraph. Leave a space between each heading for notes.
b) Write notes for each paragraph.

8. Writing Working from your notes, write a one-paragraph report on the area of research described in the article.

Unit 19 The World's Food

Listening

1. Note-making

Make full notes as you listen to each part of the talk. It is about the world's food supply. The main points covered in each part are as follows:
Part 1 The increasingly rapid growth in world population.
Part 2 Factors affecting the availability of food.
Part 3 A comparison of a high animal protein diet with one which relies mainly on vegetable protein.

2. Transferring information

Complete the following graph, which illustrates the growth of world population. Additional figures (approximate) are provided.
  1600: 500 million   1800: 100% increase   1900: 50% increase

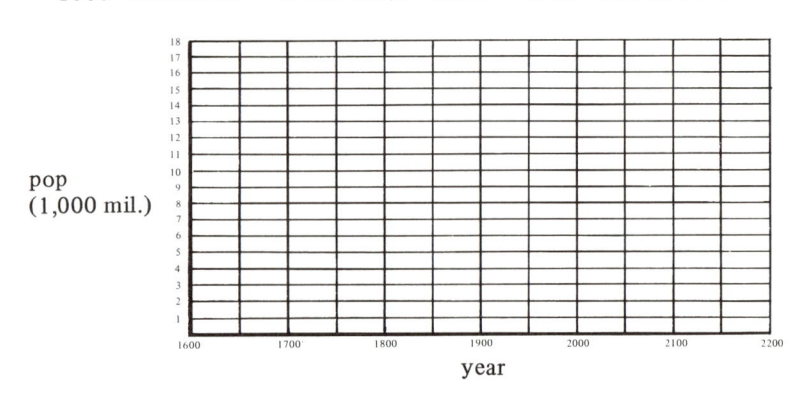

3. Note-making

List the various factors affecting food production now and in the future. Note any details mentioned.

4. Writing

Using the information given in Part 3 of the talk, together with any relevant points from Parts 1 & 2, write a short article in favour of a change to a high vegetable protein diet for people who at present eat large quantities of meat. Plan your article first in note form and only then write it out in full.

Reading

Energy, Labour and Standard of Living

Text   Para 1

1 All the operations required in crop culture can be carried out by manpower. However, producing crops by hand requires about 1000 man-hours and only about 1 ha. can be managed successfully by one person during a growing season. Under these production conditions only the bare minimum of essen-
5 tial human needs can be attained. This is because the amount of crop yield not needed for food for the farmer and thus considered surplus is extremely small. Only the surplus can be traded for other foods, goods, and services. For this reason, the standard of living achieved from most manpowered systems is relatively low when compared with that possible when mechaniza-
10 tion and large inputs of fossil fuel are used in crop production.

P2 1 Defining low and high standards of living is, at best, imprecise. In general, a relatively high standard of living includes ample food, clothing, housing, autos and numerous other material goods as well as adequate health facilities. However, a high standard of living cannot and should not necessarily be equated
5 with either contentment or happiness.

P3 1 Fossil energy can replace many man-labour inputs and the use of large supplies of relatively cheap fossil energy is a major reason a high standard of living is possible in the United States, Canada, and Europe. For example, a gallon (3.79 litres) of gasoline sells for about $0.65 in the United States. In
5 1978, based on a minimum wage of $2.65 per hour, this gallon can be purchased with only 15 minutes of work. However, that one gallon of gasoline in an engine will produce the equivalent of 97 hours of manpower. Thus, one hour of labour at $2.65 will purchase the equivalent of 395 hours of manpower in the form of fossil fuel.

P4 1 The relative prices of gasoline and labour also affect the price of food. If energy is cheap relative to the price of food, then obviously fossil energy use in food production is an excellent investment. This is true today in the United States. One thousand kilocalories of sweet corn in a can sells for about
5 $0.93 whereas 1000 kcal of gasoline has a value of $0.02. Hence, 1 kcal of sweet corn is worth 47 times more than 1 kcal of gasoline energy.

P5 1 The relationship of energy expenditure and standard of living can also be clarified by comparing production of corn by labour-intensive and energy-intensive systems. In Mexico, for instance, about 1,144 hours of manpower is expended to produce 1 ha. of corn by hand (Lewis, 1951). In the United
5 States, under an energy-intensive system, only 12 hours of labour are expended per hectare. In the midwestern United States one farmer can manage successfully up to 100 ha. of corn because he is helped by large fossil fuel inputs that run his mechanized equipment. One farmer producing corn by hand could manage only about 1.5 ha. Assuming the same profit per hectare for
10 each farmer, it is clear that the farmer managing 100 ha. will be able to support a higher standard of living.

P6 1 Thus, fossil energy has helped mankind manipulate ecosystems more effectively and efficiently for food production than ever before, and this has contributed directly to improving the standard of living in many parts of the world.   (from Pimental, D. & M. 1979: *Food, Energy and Society*)

Note   ha.   = hectare = 10 000 sq. metres
gasoline (AE) = petrol (BE)
kcal   = kilocalorie. A measure of useable energy. 1 kcal = the amount of heat needed to raise by 1°C the temperature of 1 litre of water at 15°C.

5. Content skim

a) Read the first and last paragraphs of the text. What is the general topic?
b) Read just the first sentences of paragraphs 2 – 5 (the topic sentences). What is the topic of each of these paragraphs?

6. Comprehension scan

P1.5   What does 'This' refer to?
P1.8   What does 'this' refer to?
P3.3   What does the example which follows illustrate?
P4.3   What does 'This' refer to?
P5.3   'For instance' introduces an example of what?
P5.10   What evidence makes this point clear?
P1.2   'However' is a word that signals a qualifying point. Which point is qualified and by what fact?
P2.3   Which point is qualified by 'However'?
P3.6   What contrast is made by this qualifying point?

7. Paragraph analysis — note-making

When you have checked your answers to exercise 6, study this chart. It shows in diagram form the structure of the passage, paragraph by paragraph. Compare it carefully with the passage and then fill it in. You will not have space to indicate the details of the examples, so just note the conclusion for each one. To identify conclusions, look out for signal words such as: 'thus', 'hence', etc.

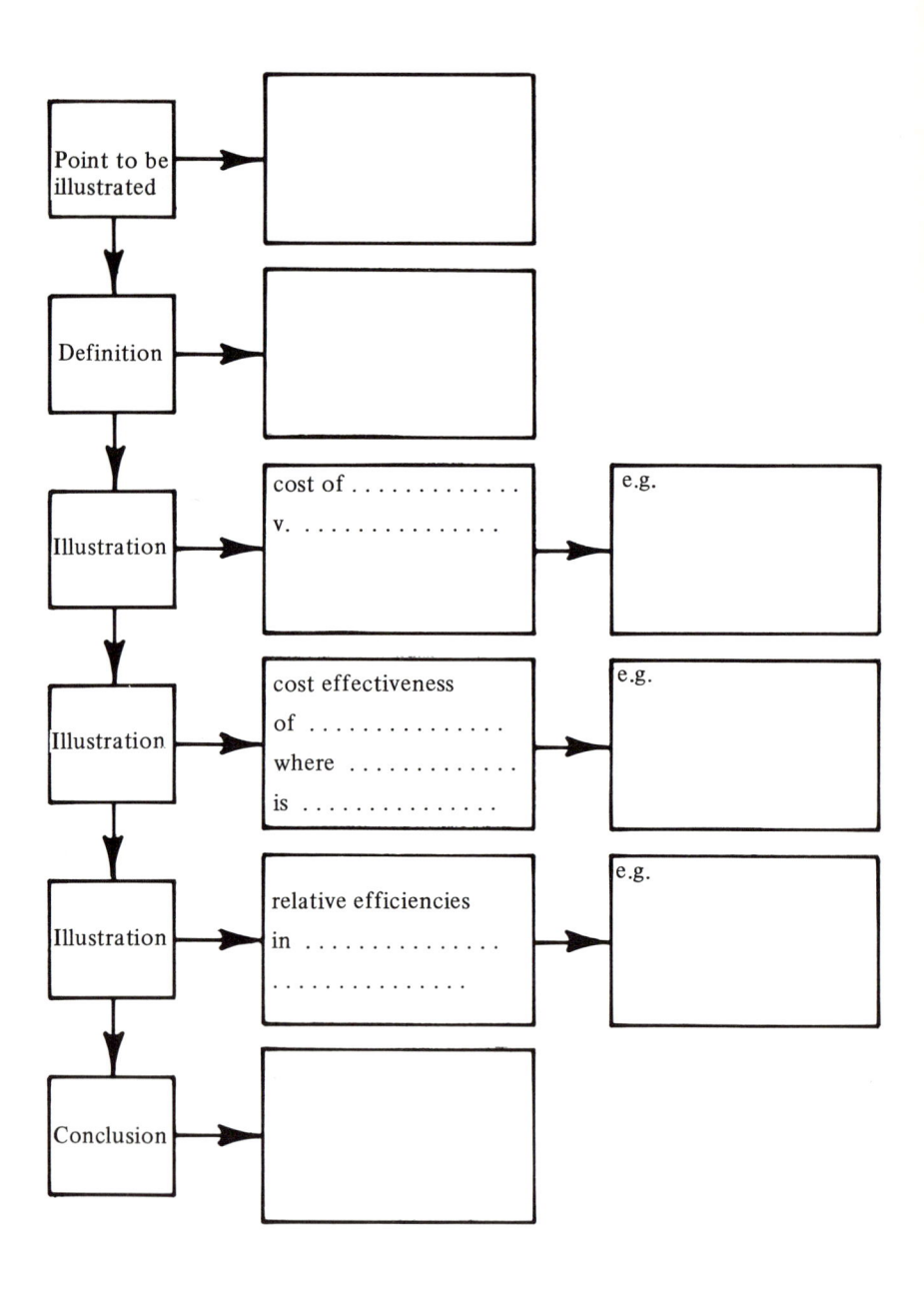

```
┌──────────────┐     ┌──────────────────┐
│ Point to be  │ ──▶ │                  │
│ illustrated  │     │                  │
└──────┬───────┘     └──────────────────┘
       ▼
┌──────────────┐     ┌──────────────────┐
│ Definition   │ ──▶ │                  │
│              │     │                  │
└──────┬───────┘     └──────────────────┘
       ▼
┌──────────────┐     ┌──────────────────┐     ┌──────────────┐
│ Illustration │ ──▶ │ cost of .......  │ ──▶ │ e.g.         │
│              │     │ v. ............  │     │              │
└──────┬───────┘     └──────────────────┘     └──────────────┘
       ▼
┌──────────────┐     ┌──────────────────┐     ┌──────────────┐
│ Illustration │ ──▶ │ cost effectiveness│ ──▶ │ e.g.         │
│              │     │ of ............  │     │              │
│              │     │ where .........  │     │              │
│              │     │ is ............  │     │              │
└──────┬───────┘     └──────────────────┘     └──────────────┘
       ▼
┌──────────────┐     ┌──────────────────┐     ┌──────────────┐
│ Illustration │ ──▶ │ relative efficiencies│▶│ e.g.         │
│              │     │ in ............  │     │              │
│              │     │ ...............  │     │              │
└──────┬───────┘     └──────────────────┘     └──────────────┘
       ▼
┌──────────────┐     ┌──────────────────┐
│ Conclusion   │ ──▶ │                  │
│              │     │                  │
└──────────────┘     └──────────────────┘
```

8. Writing

When you have completed the chart use it to write *one* paragraph summarising the general point made. You may include examples.

Unit 20   The Cinema

Listening

1. Note-making

As you listen to each part of the talk, make full notes. The talk is in three parts and deals with the early development of the cinema.

2. Note-making

Complete as much as you can of the following grid. Some names are given to help you with spellings:

Lee de Forest
W. K. L. Dickson
Auguste & Louis Lumière
Edwin Porter

Cinématographe
Kinetoscope
Technicolour

name of system, film or developer	date	sound	moving camera	length	colour	screen size	problems

3. Comparing

Using the information given so far, write briefly comparing the strong and weak points of each of the following:
a) the earliest Kinetoscope / Cinématographe
b) films like 'The Great Train Robbery' / films using de Forest's system
c) the earliest Kinetoscope / films using de Forest's system

Reading

Text

Para 1
1   In practice the range of film entertainment is wide. It tends to divide into two streams, and film study in America makes the distinction as between the *movie* and the *film*. The *movie* is for popular entertainment.[1] It is the product of an industry dominated by the producer in which there is no indivi-
5   dual film-maker but a team or unit under the producer's control. The producer hires one or more writers who complete the bulk of their work before the director is engaged to work from the script. On this the rubber stamp *final* is more than a formality: the script is not to be tampered with. The director's work is done when the shooting is finished or as a concession when
10 the first rough editing is done. The producer and editor are responsible for the final version and the director has no means of redress if he finds his intention distorted in the outcome. With their habitual precision, the French describe this kind of director (who is an interpreter like an orchestral conductor) as a *metteur-en-scène*, a term borrowed from the theatre.

P2
1   The movie is the journalism of cinema where success is measured by the quantitative response of the public. It was the mainstay of cinema during its first sixty years, particularly in the U.S.A., Britain, and Asia. Money is a vital tool in film-making and the successful movie has financed the technical innova-
5   tions from which all cinema has benefited. But it only survived by lapping up the new ideas for which every showman has to look if he is not to be left behind. These new ideas were and are being tested by the pioneers and non-conformists, the film-makers (in French, *réalisateurs*), whose work adorns the higher reaches of cinema and is described as *film*, the personal statement of
10 an author who is his own producer and director.

P3
1   The *movie* is explicit and complete in itself. Its audience is passive. The *film* is not complete: it poses implications which stimulate the audience. It involves the audience. In India the *movie* is virtually the only form of entertainment of any kind available: there is a minimal and uneconomic audience for the *film* which can only be made for export.

P4
1   *Film* (the entertainment offered to the more sophisticated) and *movie* (shown at the big, popular cinemas) vary from country to country. Some of the elements have nothing to do with aesthetics. The film in a foreign language or dialect is harder to appreciate; even if it is a British *movie*, it will be regarded by most Americans as a *film* if some of its words and all its accents are alien.[2]

P5
1   The popular audience hates to split its visual interest between the moving picture and the sub-titled translations of foreign dialogue[3] and prefers a spoken translation recorded later by a different team of actors, a process known as

---

[1] This convenient differentiation is also commercial. In Britain the number of 35mm. copies of a *movie* in circulation usually exceeds forty, while the demand by art houses for a *film* is met with five copies at most, dwindling in time to one only or even none at all.
[2] When in English there is a choice between a word of Latin derivation and one of Anglo-Saxon, the Americans prefer the former (e.g., elevator), the British prefer the latter (e.g., lift). The accent differential, too, is a real barrier in the U.S.A. It begins in New York where they say of a British film: 'Well, I got most of it', to the mid-west and beyond where they just adore your accent and then ask: 'But what exactly are you saying?'
[3] A new French process of sub-titling prints the lettering in the blank space which occurs between each frame of the picture except in anamorphic (i.e. CinemaScope) prints. But conservatism among film exhibitors inhibits them from changing the shape of the screen to accommodate the new position of the titling.

dubbing.[4] To the minority this is sacrilege, though they unwittingly accept it in nearly every film from Italy, where it is customary for actors to speak in their own language and for Italian speech to be dubbed over their lip movements after the film has been edited. To see and hear a performance from the same actor is rare in an Italian picture.[5]
(from Dickinson, T. 1971: *A Discovery of Cinema*)

[4] As a film editor I used dubbing as early as 1932. In the first case, to remove an inadequate sub-plot from a completed film, I dubbed new dialogue, spoken by the leading lady, over some of her close-ups in order to bridge the gaps in the story. When audiences failed to notice this, I improved an inadequate performance in another film by synchronizing the actress's best visual performance with the speech from shots in which she had spoken her lines better. Some reviewers singled out this synthesis as one of the best performances in the film.
[5] See 'Italy Sotto Voce', *Sight and Sound*, vol. 37, no. 3, p. 146.

4. Content skim   Read the first three sentences of P1 and the first sentence of each subsequent paragraph. What is the topic of the passage?

5. Comprehension scan
P1.1   What does 'It' refer to?
P1.4   In which case would you expect there to be an individual film maker?
P1.7   What does 'this' refer to?
P1.10 What has happened to the film before it reaches its final version?
P1.12 What situation does the phrase 'in the outcome' refer to?
P1.12 Who is referred to by 'their'?
P2.5   What main kinds of film are included in 'all cinema'?

6. Sequencing   Using the information in P1, draw a flowchart showing the main steps in the making of a movie. It may help you to answer these questions first:
a) What does the writer write?
b) What is the director's job?

7. Describing   Indicate on the lines of the two arrows how the movie and the film support each other.

```
┌─────────┐  ←─────────  ┌─────────┐
│  Movie  │              │  Film   │
│         │  ─────────→  │         │
└─────────┘              └─────────┘
```

8. Contrasting   What is the main difference between the ways films and movies are made?

9. Contrasting   In P3, what contrast does the writer make between the movie and the film?

10. Comparing   In two columns, headed *Movie* and *Film,* write words or phrases showing the differences the author finds between them.

11. Writing   Write a paragraph explaining simply the contrast the writer makes between the movie and the film.

Tapescript

Note: In order to simulate a lecture theatre, the talks were recorded under authentic conditions. The tapescript is a faithful transcription of the talks and therefore retains the occasional slight inaccuracies which are a normal feature of spoken language.

Unit 3   Earthquakes

Part 1
An earthquake is a shaking movement or tremor on the surface of the earth. Some are so slight that we need sensitive instruments to detect them while the most severe can cause terrible destruction. Most earthquakes, especially large ones, are caused by a fracture or splitting of the earth's crust. This happens when the stress on the rocks becomes greater than their strength. These stresses originate in the mantle or are the result of slow movements in the continental plates, the thick parts of the outer crust. Earthquakes can also occur in association with volcanoes and some are caused by drilling and pumping deep in the ground.

Part 2
Most earthquakes occur in the crust but others are deep-focussed, originating in the mantle, because of the movement of solid material in this otherwise semi-fluid layer. The depth at which an earthquake originates, that is its focus, can be located by measuring the timing of the shock waves. There are two main kinds of wave: the preliminary and the surface waves. The preliminary waves are again divided into primary and secondary types. Both types travel at different speeds depending on their depth, but secondary waves travel at an overall speed of about half that of the primary type. By measuring the length of time between the arrival of each kind of preliminary wave, scientists can estimate the location of the focus of the earthquake.

Part 3
Earthquakes are measured on instruments called seismographs. The best-known system of measurement is the Richter — R-I-C-H-T-E-R — scale. In addition, there is the Mercalli, spelt M-E-R-C-A-double-L-I, scale, in which the strength of the earthquake is estimated by the amount of damage it does to man-made structures. To give some examples, a Point four earthquake on the Mercalli scale would cause small objects like plates to shake and it might cause movement in door and window frames. A Point five earthquake would overturn stable objects like tall vases or table lamps. At Point six, slight damage to buildings would occur. At Point eight, chimneys and other tall constructions such as statues in public places would fall and there would be a good deal of damage to ordinary buildings. A Point ten earthquake would result in severe damage and at Point twelve, the highest on the Mercalli scale, damage would be total and the shock waves would be large enough to be easily visible on the surface of the ground.

Unit 4   Energy Sources

Part 1
All forms of non-renewable energy sources are to a greater or lesser extent polluting, though the type of pollution varies. Coal, in common with other fossil fuels, produces sulphur dioxide, though in this respect gas compares very favourably with coal and oil. The combustion of fossil fuels also produces carbon dioxide in far greater quantities than plant life can use. This carbon dioxide, by accumulating in the atmosphere, may well lead to global rises in temperature (called the 'greenhouse effect') and such rises could in time have a disastrous effect on climate. Nuclear fuel does not emit gases into the atmosphere when used, but it produces its own highly toxic waste products. Being solid, these are easier to control than the gases emitted by fossil fuels but their presence in growing quantities is potentially very dangerous indeed. All forms of fuel so far mentioned add to the earth's heat load and in this way provide a long-term danger to the environment. The wide availability of fossil fuels, on the other hand, and the increasing availability of nuclear sources inevitably ensure that they will go on being fully exploited for as long as they can last.

Part 2
Our total reserves of fossil fuels are equivalent to about two days' supply of solar energy. So, there is enough energy from the sun for everybody, but its low intensity makes it very difficult to use in terms of cost, efficiency and continuous availability in any one place. On the other hand, it is going to be possible for solar sources to be developed sufficiently to make this form of power very important in the coming decades. The obvious advantages of solar power over fossil fuels are that it is non-finite — or, in our terms, renewable; it creates no pollution and it does not add to the earth's heat load.

Part 3

Geothermal power has been referred to in your reading and, as you learned there, it is unlikely ever to be of very major importance. Water or hydro-power, on the other hand, is likely to make a real contribution to future needs in terms of renewable sources. Some forms depend on natural waterfalls or the building of dams. These are likely to be very limited in availability, since the building of a dam can have serious effects on the locality in terms of the loss of agricultural land, the silting up of rivers and even changes in climate. The seas, on the other hand, can be exploited by using the tides or waves. This source has a much greater availability but it is hardly practicable to build a dam across every estuary to contain the high tide, nor to cover our seas with equipment for gathering energy from the waves. In this respect, wave power has some of the dis-advantages as solar power — that is, the equipment needed takes up a great deal of space. Although, therefore, there are real drawbacks to the use of some of these sources — including the risk of altering the environment in a harmful way — they will no doubt be developed as far as possible. Of course, they all possess the advantages of being non-polluting and of not adding to the earth's heat load.

Unit 5 The Whale

Part 1

The earliest people to engage in whaling in an organized way were the Basques, who began to exploit the right whale in the north Atlantic in the twelfth and thirteenth centuries. They would go from the shore in boats, harpoon small whales and return with their catch to land. This kind of whaling spread to northern grounds, where it was taken up by the Dutch, English and Norwegians. In the eighteenth and nineteenth centuries, the United States of America became a major whaling nation, working in the Indian Ocean and the Pacific. Their bases were large ocean-going vessels which could stay at sea for up to five years and the whales, caught from smaller boats, were cut up on deck and the oil stored below. During the same period, whaling stations were established in the Antarctic harbours from which boats would go out, make their catch and return, so that the whales could be processed on shore.

Part 2

During the nineteenth century, steamships became common and the explosive harpoon gun was invented. These developments made it possible to catch larger species, such as the blue whale. In the present century, whaling has become a highly sophisticated activity. Factory ships have been developed which can process and store all the usable products of a catch, and aids such as spotter planes and radar have made it much easier to trace and follow whales in the oceans. Unfortunately, such techniques have depleted certain species of whale alarmingly. The estimated population of the blue whale was fourteen thousand five hundred in the nineteen thirties. By nineteen sixty-eight there were only six hundred left. This species, along with certain others, is now heavily protected, but commercial pressures and insensitivity to the environment have done much to hinder the progress of conservation measures. In protecting their own whaling industries, some nations will eventually destroy those same industries by destroying the whales on which they depend.

Part 3

The International Whaling Commission was established in nineteen forty-eight to regulate whaling throughout the world. Twenty-four nations belong to it. Many people doubt the effectiveness of this body, which may achieve no more than to slow down the inevitable extinction of some species. It has imposed some restrictions but almost certainly not enough. In nineteen seventy-two the UN Conference on the Environment recommended a ten-year moratorium on whaling to allow stocks to build up again. The IWC has still not heeded this advice. At its thirty-second annual conference in July nineteen eighty, a majority voted for a complete moratorium, but the necessary three-quarters majority was not obtained, so the proposal was not adopted. It failed also to agree to stop hunting the sperm whale or to set a quota on the bowhead, another diminishing species. Eventually the Commission agreed only to reduce the quota for Antarctic whaling. Many critics felt that the Commission, by its inability to act decisively, was taking the world one step nearer to the destruction, not only of the whaling industry but of the whale itself.

Unit 6 Silicon Chips

Part 1

Now, each wafer is polished on one side until the surface is extremely smooth. This is the side on which the circuits of each chip will be built up. The wafers are then baked in a very hot tubular furnace, as you can see in diagram five. Right. This produces a layer of silicon oxide on the surface of each wafer. Silicon oxide will not conduct electricity, so the surface of each wafer is now an insulator, while the silicon on the inside remains a semi-conductor. A special photographic film called a photo-mask is now made. Diagram six shows a cross-section of this. This is the same size as the wafer and has printed on it one layer of the correct micro-circuit. One for each chip will be made from the wafer. Parts of the photo-mask will allow ultra-violet light to pass through and others will not. The wafer is then coated with a, a chemical substance called photo-resist which becomes hard when ultra-violet light falls on it. Now, if you look at diagram seven, there, see that. The photo-mask is placed over the wafer and it is exposed to ultra-violet light. The photo-resist not exposed to UV light remains soft and this is then washed off with acid, as you can see in diagrams nine and ten. Next the layer of silicon oxide underneath the soft photo-resist is washed off and finally the hard photo-resist is removed. The surface of each chip on the wafer now shows the pattern of the circuit where the silicon is exposed. surrounded by the remaining silicon oxide. Now for these steps, you want to look at diagrams ten to twelve.

Part 2
In order to make the transistor, certain parts of the silicon must now have added to them the second chemical impurity. This is done by placing the wafer in another furnace containing the second chemical in the form of a gas. The chemical cannot penetrate the silicon oxide but it enters the areas of exposed silicon, as you can see in diagram thirteen. So now each chip on the wafer consists of two kinds of silicon and a partial surface of oxide. The shape of the circuit, formed by the surrounding oxide, is now filled in with a metal. This is done by exposing the wafer to the vapour of the relevant metal, which is usually aluminum*. One complete layer of transistors with their connections has now been manufactured. Other layers are then added by a similar process until a complete chip is built (*American English).

Part 3
Each chip is next tested by a machine to find out if it is working correctly. Because the components are very small, even with modern methods as many as eighty-five per cent of the chips on a wafer may be useless. Fortunately, because the process is cheap, this does not matter too much. Next, the wafer is cut up into individual chips and the faulty ones are rejected. Each functioning chip is then mounted in a protective package and tiny wires are fixed to each of its contacts so it can be incorporated into a computer, watch, television game, cash register, factory robot or any of the vast number of electronic units in which chips are now employed.

Unit 7   Rubber

Part 1
You have read of how latex is removed from the rubber tree by the simple process of tapping. Now you will hear how that latex is converted into the raw rubber which provides the basic material for a multitude of end products.

But first, what is latex, this whitish, milky liquid? Its composition is relatively simple. It consists chiefly of water. In that water, in solution, there are small amounts of sugars, inorganic salts and proteins. Moving through the liquid by Brownian motion are minute globules of rubber. When I say 'minute' I am referring to a globule one sixteen-thousandth of an inch in diameter. These rubber particles make up a third to two fifths of the weight of the latex, that is to say, they contribute thirty to forty percent of the overall weight of the juice.

Part 2
That, then, is what latex consists of. The first part of the process of extracting raw rubber from latex is coagulation. Coagulation — that's C-O-A-G-U-L-A-T-I-O-N, OK? means making a liquid thicken by clotting, that is, by bringing parts of the liquid together in solid or semi-solid pieces, and this is what happens to the rubber globules in the latex. A solid clot of rubber is formed by the addition of acids or salts to the latex.

The first part of the coagulation stage is the straining of the latex to remove any particles of dirt which it contains. Next, the latex is poured into tanks. An equal amount of water is added to the latex to produce a diluted mixture. Finally, acetic or formic acid, or sodium silicofluoride, is added to bring about coagulation. All this, by the way, must be done within twenty-four hours of the latex being collected, otherwise it may go off and become useless.

Part 3
So coagulation, as we have seen, is the first step in the process of deriving rubber from latex. I have already described how clots of rubber are formed when salts or acids are added to the diluted latex.

This stage is completed in special tanks which are designed to produce bars or slabs of rubber. The tanks are divided up by a series of aluminium partitions. As coagulation takes place, the rubber rises to the surface of the tank and sets between the aluminium dividers.

The soft, thick, substance which coagulates in the tanks is coagulum, spelled C-O-A-G-U-L-U-M. This is now washed and pressed between heavy rollers to remove liquid and dirt.

The coagulum can now be processed in one of two ways, depending on the type of rubber to be produced. There are two types, smoked sheet and pale crepe, spelled C-R-E-P-E.

Smoked sheet is the more commonly produced type. To produce it, the last pair of rollers at the processing stage are ribbed, and they roll out sheet rubber one tenth of an inch thick. This is cut up into suitable lengths, hung, and smoked in a smoke-house for a period of seven days.

The second, less common, type, pale crepe, is produced when slabs of coagulum are passed through heavy corrugated rollers which revolve at different speeds. Pale crepe gets its pale yellow colour by the addition of small amounts of sodium bisulphite and acetic acid. It isn't smoke dried, but hung in large sheds and air dried.

Only after these initial steps is the rubber ready for further industrial processing and manufacture. And with aspects of that we shall deal next week.

Unit 8   Volcanoes

Part 1

What is a volcano? My dictionary defines it as 'a centre <u>of eruption</u> of subterranean matter, typically a more or less conical hill or mountain, built <u>of ash or lava,</u> with a central crater and pipe'. That's a description which will confirm the image which many of us who do not come from volcanic regions of the world have of a typical volcano, a cone beautiful in <u>its symmetry</u>, and with a wisp of 'smoke' rising from its summit. You and I know that 'smoke' is no such thing, of course. <u>It's escaping steam,</u> dust and gases.

But this of course, is a gross over-simplification. Volcanoes assume many different shapes <u>according to</u> the type of volcanic activity which has constructed them. And they change shape, too. When the Bezymianny Volcano on the Kamchatka Peninsula <u>erupted in</u> nineteen fifty-five, two hundred metres of the summit <u>were blown off</u>, and a major part of the side of its crater collapsed. So it's not feasible to try to categorise volcanoes by their shapes. What we can do is postulate different types according to <u>the site of</u> eruption on a volcano.

Part 2

The Mount Fuji type is that of a summit eruption. Here the gas and ash are blown up and away from the crater at the top of the volcano, and the lava runs down the mountain-side from the summit crater. Then, it is possible for the explosion of the gases to take place at the summit, but for the bulk of the lava to be ejected through a vent on the side of the mountain. This is a flank eruption. In another type, the summit is fairly, but not entirely, quiet, and the main site of the eruption is again on the flank of the mountain. This lateral eruption differs from a flank eruption in that a small cone is built up on the side of the volcano. The final type is similar to the lateral, except that there is no summit activity at all. A new cone builds up, sometimes dwarfing the parent volcano which fed it. This is known as a parasitic eruption.

Now, I want you to examine the volcano outlines, and decide to which of the categories each belongs. The billowing clouds represent the escaping gases, the stream-like shapes, the lava running down the volcano's slopes. Mark the summit eruption 'A', the flank eruption 'B' and the lateral and parasitic eruptions 'C' and 'D' respectively. Oh, there is one outline which does not belong to any of these types. Mark that 'X'.

Part 3

We've looked at some different types of volcano classified by the site of their eruptions. Now we are going to consider different types of eruption classified according to different criteria, such as their relative strength, lava type, and so on. By doing this we shall be able to compare and contrast the Hawaiian type of eruption with the Strombolian and Vulcanian. We should not forget that there are different types of eruption, rather than of volcano. In other words, although one volcano may be categorised by one type of eruption, it may well erupt in more than one way.

The Hawaiian eruption, named after the Hawaiian Islands of the Pacific, is the gentlest type. The Hawaiian Islands stand on a mid-ocean ridge and their lavas are entirely basaltic. They are, therefore, extremely hot and fluid. This enables the gas in the magma below the volcano to escape with ease, and there are no violent explosions, therefore, in this type of eruption. The lavas escape quietly, and are erupted semi-continuously. Sometimes, when the lava is erupted from a deep crater from which it cannot escape, lava lakes are formed, and spectacular lava fountains are blown off during eruptions, sometimes as high as four hundred metres.

Like the Hawaiian eruption, the Strombolian is comparatively gentle and safe. Named after the Italian island volcano of Stromboli, this type, too, erupts basaltic lava, although of a rather less fluid kind than the Hawaiian. Similarly, Strombolian eruptions are more or less continuous, the volcanoes rumbling gently on for long periods. Because the lava is less fluid, the gases in it do not escape with the ease of the Hawaiian, but they do escape every few minutes in a rush of noise. Strombolian volcanoes are, indeed, noisier than Hawaiian. The explosions throw out semi-solid lava which solidifies around the vent, or bounce downhill as cooling rocks, but never very far. As with the Hawaiian, the volume of ejected gas, steam and ash is slight relative to the more explosive types of eruption.

A Vulcanian eruption is such a type. Vulcano, on the Lipari Islands in the Mediterranean has given its name in English to all volcanoes. A Vulcanian eruption occurs only infrequently in the life of a volcano, unlike the semi-constant Hawaiian and Strombolian types. When it does, however, it may continue for many months. Its lava is much less fluid than that of the other types, and it is old, solidified lava which has been blocking the volcanic vent which is erupted. In contrast to the Hawaiian and Strombolian, these eruptions are violent, often so violent that part of the volcano is destroyed. And being violent and irregular, naturally, a Vulcanian eruption can be dangerous. It can fling great blocks of material large distances, and often gives off a large cloud of choking gas and ash which can rise several kilometres into the sky.

A Vulcanian eruption, then, is awesome in its power and capacity to damage. Here we will conclude, although I might just end by adding that there are another three types of eruption greater than the Vulcanian.

Unit 9   Function

Part 1

In our everyday life we are surrounded by instructions; <u>so much so</u> that we fail to realise just how many, and just how automatic is our response to most of them. There are differences in content and form, of course. Some <u>are stronger</u> than others; it's safe to ignore some, but not others.

<u>Just think</u> for a moment how my day begins, and probably yours too. <u>If I travel</u> to work by car, I am bombarded by commands in the form of coloured lights, signs, symbols and numerals. If I go by train, <u>I am told</u> to show my ticket, <u>whether or not</u> I can smoke, not to stick my head out of the window. When I arrive at College, a notice tells me that I must show my identity card to get in.

<u>These are all examples</u> of simple instructions. Notice, by the way, that I have been using 'instruction' <u>loosely</u>, in the idiomatic way, to mean the same as 'order'. <u>Used in the sense of</u> telling someone how to do something that was our earlier, stricter, definition it brings us back to the idea of instruction <u>as a set of</u> sequential orders, often given with reasons. Recipes tell us how to cook and bake, patterns to knit and sew, maps how to get from A to B. <u>And every</u> gadget we buy, from a tin-opener to a microcomputer, comes complete with instructions we <u>must refer to to</u> make the equipment function properly. So being able to follow (and give) instructions is vital. And since the function of instructing is often realised by imperatives, you are now going to be given a couple of exercises in following instructions.

Part 2

First, we'll look at a way of describing spatial relations within a rectangular area. You may want to identify the position of something on the board, or tell someone where to put things on the floor or the wall of your room, or just describe the different parts which make up a painting.

Have a look at the first figure. Draw a line from the top left dot to the top right, passing through the middle two. Do the same with the row of dots at the bottom. Right? Next, join up the sides; draw a line from the top left to the bottom left dot passing through the two middle dots on that side. Do the same for the right-hand side. Now, join the dot one-third of the way down the right-hand side to the dot one-third of the way down the left-hand side. OK? Do the same now with the dots two-thirds of the way down the sides of the figure.

Well, if you've got that, you should now have a rectangle, in fact it's a square, containing two lines parallel to the top. These lines divide the rectangle into three horizontal sections. Finally, join up the last four dots so they divide the rectangle into three equal vertical sections. What you have should now be a rectangle divided into nine equal rectangular parts.

OK, have you all got that? Next, let's name these parts. The middle section's easy. Write that in — middle section. Then there are four corners. Identify those. Write 'corner' in each one. OK, but we want to distinguish between them. There are two top and two bottom. Write 'top' above the two top corners, but leave a space between the words 'top' and 'corner'. The same now for the bottom two, but writing 'bottom' instead of 'top', of course. Now we have to distinguish between the two top and two bottom corners. Write 'left-hand' between 'top' and 'corner' in that corner, so that we have finally labelled it 'top left-hand corner'. Do the same for the bottom left-hand corner. Last, give the two remaining corners their labels. OK? We're left with four . . . sections, let's call them — and they're all between corners, so let's call these 'middle', or better still, 'mid-' —M-I-D-HYPHEN— sections. Mid-sections. Write that in all four spaces. Finish off by naming the top mid-section, the bottom mid-section, the left-hand and the right-hand.

Part 3

Well, if you've survived so far, let's try another short exercise in following instructions, a little more complex this time. Look at the second figure. Draw a circle in the bottom left-hand corner, its circumference touching all four sides of that corner section. Do the same again in the bottom right-hand corner. Right, have you got that? OK. Now, from the centre of the bottom left-hand corner circle, draw a line to the top right-hand right angle of that corner section. Listen carefully, a line going from the centre of the circle to the top right-hand corner of that corner section. Next, draw a line from the centre of the bottom right circle to the top left right angle of that particular corner section. OK? Now join the two lines by drawing along the dotted line which divides the middle section of the figure from its bottom mid-section. Having done that, place a dot in the centre of the bottom mid-section. That's it, a dot marking the centre of the bottom mid-section. Then, draw a line from that dot to the top right right-angle of that section. Draw another line to the top left right-angle of the bottom mid-section. Now, draw a line to half way up the dotted line which divides the left-hand mid-section from the middle section. OK. Still there? Good. Draw a semi-circle starting from the top of the line you have just drawn which finishes half way down that line. Can you see what you're drawing now? If it's beginning to look like a means of transport, you're on the right lines, as we say. Right, finally, draw half way up the dotted line which divides the middle section from the right-hand mid-section. Finish by drawing a line of about one centimetre from the top of that line towards the centre of the middle section, at ninety degrees. Got it? OK. What have you drawn? Finish it off by drawing in the driving wheel, chain and pedals.

Unit 10   Kalahari Bushmen

Part 1

Every language has its paralanguage, that's to say, it has a system of non-verbal communication — one in which gestures or sounds take the place of words. Probably the most complex paralanguage, although you might argue with me for describing it as such, is the artificially developed one used by the deaf. That, of course, is a system designed to replicate spoken language as fully as possible, but with signs replacing the spoken word. Natural paralanguage, however, is used to extend language, or as a substitute for it when circumstances do not permit it to be used effectively.

Paralanguage can be divided into three main categories of use. First, gesture is used to communicate at distances greater than those over which words can carry. Think of how you wave an arm, or both arms, to attract the attention of someone out of earshot. Communicating over a distance, naturally, requires expansive gestures.

Non-verbal sound too, is used, as in the whistle 'languages' of the Basques and the islanders of La Gomera in the Canaries. The higher frequency of the whistled note carries for long distances in their mountainous homes.

Paralanguage is also used to convey a message in silence when that is important or desirable. We will often nod or shake our head rather than speak, and laying a finger on the lips is probably a universal gesture enjoining silence. To those expert hunters, the Kalahari Bushmen, silence is vital when prey is being stalked, and they have evolved a wide vocabulary of gestures by which one hunter can describe which animal he has seen to an unsighted companion. And then there are those occasions when a gesture or facial expression is used because the economy and force of a physical movement can be far more expressive than any string of words; 'her look spoke volumes' we say in English.

The third use of paralanguage is complementary to language, that is gesture or noise used to lend additional meaning to what is being said, to emphasize or perhaps even to contradict; a wink indicates that the speaker is not serious, for example, or the tongue thrust in the cheek, although I have a feeling that that last example is now rather old-fashioned.

Part 2

While paralanguage is universal, there are differences in its forms across cultures. In Western societies, for example, a person who wishes to signal 'Come here!' will crook his or her forefinger, or cup a hand with the fingers upward, and move it towards the body. In certain Near and Far Eastern societies the hand is cupped also, but with the fingers pointing downwards. Confusion may arise between members of these different cultures, as the 'Come here!' gesture in which the fingers point down looks remarkably like the gesture which indicates 'Go away!' to Western eyes.

Ways of counting on the fingers also vary. A Western person will strike each finger of one hand with the forefinger of the other as the numbers are counted. This is also found in many countries of the Middle and Near East, but then so is the method in which the thumb of one hand is tapped against each finger of that hand, finishing with the thumb placed in the centre of the palm on the count of five.

Before we conclude by examining a few of the sign 'words' of the Bushmen, let's just check that you are familiar with the names in English of the different fingers of the hand by getting you to label that picture in your workbook. You must know the thumb, the thickest of the fingers, there, on the left. On the other side of the hand is the little finger — it's easy to see why it's so-named. And what about the three fingers in between. The one next to the thumb is the fore — F-O-R-E- finger, all one word. That, of course, is our pointing finger, and it's also known as the index finger. Next to that is the middle finger, and between the middle and little finger is the third finger.

Part 3

Now, let's finish by looking at six sign words from the paralanguage of the hunter-gatherers of the Kalahari Desert. Look at the six pictures and decide which each type represents. Each one, by the way, indicates a different type of animal, but I'll tell you which once you've identified the different signs.
Type A: the thumb and forefinger are opened, forming a shape just like a horsehoe lying on its side. The other three fingers are clenched against the palm.
Type B: the hand and lower arm are used. The arm is curved at elbow and wrist. The fingers are pressed together and bent downwards from the upper knuckles.
Type C: the fore- and middle fingers are raised in a 'V', with the third and little fingers pressed down against the curved thumb.
Type D: the hand is raised palm-outwards, and pressed back against the wrist. The five fingers are raised, separated and slightly crooked.
Type E: the hand is made into a fist with the knuckles and back of the hand uppermost, but the thumb and little finger are separated from the other

three and point forwards.
Type F: the open palm is held up with the fingers separated and straight, except for the middle finger which is pointed forwards almost at right-angles to the others.

Well, if you have identified the different types successfully you will see now how extraordinarily expressive they are. Complete your classification by writing the name of the animal which the sign represents under the appropriate picture. Sign A means 'hawk', B 'ostrich', C 'hare', D 'porcupine', E 'giraffe' and F 'lion'.

Unit 11   The Camera

Part 1
This afternoon we are going to find out how to develop an ordinary black and white film. So first we'll look at what we need — what equipment and chemicals, I mean — and after that look at each step in the process. Remember, we're only talking about developing photographic film. Printing the photographs will come later.

So first of all, <u>what do we need</u>? Well, this is the equipment here. As I'm showing it, you write in the names of the pieces against the illustrations which you've got <u>in front of</u> you. We'll start with the developing tank, which is where most of the action takes place; that's where we put the film and the chemicals. <u>This one here</u> on my left is a stainless steel tank. It's dear compared to the plastic type, but it'll last much longer. Here on my right, that's your left, of course, <u>we've got a</u> couple of measuring instruments. There's a thermometer, <u>because</u> in black and white development it's important to keep the chemicals' temperature on twenty degrees centigrade. Then this here is a timer. I find it easier to see than my watch. That beaker behind it is a measurer too — <u>we've got to</u> measure our chemicals out accurately. Finally, a rubber tube and water filter to wash the film after <u>it's been developing in</u> the chemicals, and, oh yes, these at the very front are clips, used to hang the film up to dry. I like this plastic sort myself, because they don't go rusty like their metal ones.

Well, that's the hardware; <u>what about the</u> chemicals? We only need three. The developer — it's an alkaline solution — comes in powder form, so we've got to add water. You can get it as <u>a concentrated liquid</u>, but it's much dearer that way, so my advice is, don't bother. The stop bath is <u>an acid solution</u>, which means it stops the developer's action straight away, and that helps to guard against over-development. Last, there's the fixer, which fixes or sets the film.

Part 2
Now then, how is it done? The tank is loaded like this. Be careful always to hold the film by the edges, or you'll spoil it. And the film is put into the reel ... like ... so. Ah! Of course, the film has been taken out of the cassette to start with, and removed from the backing paper. And I should have said that before the tank is loaded, it's important to check the temperature of the chemicals. See that it's twenty centigrade. Now, the developer is poured in — quickly, so as to prevent uneven development, and the timer is started. Development has begun.

Part 3
Now that development has started, keep a careful eye on the timer. There will be instructions with the film you're developing about just how long you've got to give it. As soon as you've finished pouring the developer into the tank you should start shaking it like this continuously for the first half minute. After that, turn the tank upside down each minute until the film has completed the recommended development time. When time is up, pour the developer away, back into the bottle, I mean. Next, pour in the stop bath as quickly as you can — its acid will halt the alkaline action of the developer. Shake the tank for another minute, then replace the stop bath in its bottle. Waste not, want not, I always say. Next, pour in the fixer and agitate — give it a good shake like this for the first thirty seconds. When the fixing time is over, couple the tank up to your darkroom tap. Use your rubber tube for that. You can relax for a bit now, because the film has to be washed for half an hour. Finally, remove the film from its tank and hang it up to dry. Suspend it from a line by those plastic clips. Now, let's go and try to put all this theory into practice. Ready?

Unit 12   Pliny and Pompeii

Part 1
The houses of well-to-do families in Pompeii and Herculaneum varied in size, number of rooms and layout, but nevertheless displayed many features in common. A typical house of the first century B.C. consisted of <u>one storey</u> only, but had an area of, say, <u>six hundred and fifty to seven hundred and fifty square metres</u>. Outside, the roof was generally flat, and the walls brightly painted. The walls were blank, windowless, except possibly for some small windows in the sides, but <u>decorative pillars</u> flanked the doors.

Like traditional houses in the Middle East today, the houses were inward-looking. The main entrance was <u>through a corridor</u> divided by a door. The outer part of the corridor was the vestibulum, V-E-S-T-I-B-U-L-U-M, which has given us the English 'vestibule', still in use today; the inner vestibule was the fauces, F-A-U-C-E-S. At the end of the fauces the house <u>opened out into</u> a hall open to the sky. In the centre of this hall, the atrium, that's A-T-R-I-U-M, a tank stored rainwater. The shrine where the household gods were worshipped <u>was usually situated in</u>

the corner of the atrium.

Two small rooms, alae, spelled A-L-A-E, or <u>wings</u>, separated the outer from the inner part of the house. The main room, the tablinum, T-A-B-L-I-N-U-M, <u>looked on to the</u> atrium or hall. The tablinum originally functioned as the reception and dining room, and often as the main bedroom too. Larger houses, however, also had separate dining rooms. The triclinium, dining room, that's T-R-I-C-L-I-N-I-U-M, was generally small, however, too small <u>for anything but</u> family eating or very small-scale entertainment. Finally, at the far end of the house, could be found the peristyle – peristylum in Latin – P-E-R-I-S-T-Y-L-U-M, – <u>a walled garden</u>, frequently colonnaded, that is, with a row, or rows, of columns around it. Bedrooms were to be found in different parts of the house, <u>often off</u> the atrium.

Part 2
The oldest house in ruined Pompeii is that known to us as the House of the Surgeon. Its design is simple and symmetrical. It lies on a north-east south-west axis. The northern corner is taken up by the peristyle, the walled garden. The south and west corners, the rooms on either side of the entrance, housed shops, a feature common to many of the larger houses of the doomed city.

The entrance was not divided into an inner and outer vestibule; the main door gives on to a short, relatively wide, corridor, beyond which is the atrium. That is flanked by four bedrooms, two on each side. The two inner bedrooms are approximately of the same dimensions as the wings immediately beyond them.

In the inner part of the house this symmetry is continued. The tablinum opens directly on to the atrium. To both right and left are dining rooms, the larger to the right. And so, having described the principal living areas of the House of the Surgeon, we need trouble ourselves no further with those of lesser importance.

UNIT 13 Lasers and Holograms

Part 1
Holography, the production of three-dimensional <u>photographic images</u>, is the result of one application of the laser. In fact, Dennis Gabor, the inventor of holography first <u>conceived of it</u> in 1948 as a way of improving the electron microscope. Various difficulties rendered this idea <u>impracticable</u>, however, until the development of the laser. Gabor was awarded the Nobel Prize for Physics twenty-three years after <u>he had first thought</u> of the possibilities of the hologram.

A hologram (Gabor's coinage) is a 'total recording' of the optical information <u>in a light wave front</u>. The image of an object is recorded on a medium such as a photographic plate or transparency by the use of laser light, and the image of an apparently real object <u>is reconstructed</u> when a laser beam is played upon the 'exposed' recording medium. Let's take a look in <u>a bit more detail</u> at the processes involved in the making of a hologram, and the creation of a holographic image.

Part 2
We shall consider how a hologram of a static object is made, for which a continuous wave laser is used. In a darkened room, a laser beam is directed at an object some distance from it. That's the laser, to the left in the diagram. The object 'O' to be recorded is on the right. The object in the background is a mirror, and the recording medium, the photographic transparency, let us say, in the foreground.

Part 3
The laser light directed on to the object is diffracted by it on to the transparency. At the same time, part of the laser beam is divided off and directed on to the mirror as a reference beam. This beam is also reflected on to the transparency. In the course of this re-direction the two beams, one coming back from the object, the other from the mirror, interfere with each other. Now, the resulting 'interference fringes', as they are known, are imprinted on the recording medium. This record in no way resembles the object; what is produced is a pattern, a pattern of banded and swirling shapes. But it is a complete record of the amplitude and phase characteristics of the interference fringes. The transparency, therefore, records the information of the amplitude of the fringes, that is, the variations in the depths of the waves, as well as the phase information. By phase information we mean information about the variations in their position relative to each other, or rather, the extent to which the wave fronts are coherent – in step. When they are in phase, crest matching crest, and so on, the recorded images are light. And when they are out of phase, the fringes leave a dark image.

Part 4
Now, to produce the holographic image, a laser is again required. The laser beam is directed on to the recording medium, and the major part of it passes straight through in the form of extraneous light. The remainder, however, is diffracted by the interference fringes recorded on the plate. This results in a reversal of the conditions under which the information was recorded.

Two images are produced at different angles to the transparency, both three-dimensional because they reproduce phase and amplitude information on the waves of the original. A 'virtual' image appears between the laser and the transparency. On the far side of the transparency a 'real' image is produced. This image, unlike the virtual, can be photographed and examined by microscope. In the real image, the parallax relationships are the reverse of those of the original, but this problem can be overcome by a double hologram.

To the layman, the hologram must be one of the most magical of the developments of modern science. Nor will that impression be dispelled by the knowledge that if the recording medium which stores the optical information about the properties of an object is damaged, or partly destroyed, sufficient information is stored to enable the perfect reproduction of the object.

Unit 14   Sleep and Dreams

Part 1

<u>If I were to ask</u> everyone of you in this lecture hall what you dreamed about last night, I know the sort <u>of responses</u> I would get. <u>Some would</u> say they had not dreamed of anything, adding, perhaps, that they never dream. <u>Others would describe</u> rather ordinary and unexciting dreams: the common dream, for example, of re-experiencing <u>some of the events</u> of the previous day. Some of you would report strange and colourful dreams, of bizarre happenings <u>in unconnected</u> sequences, a type of dream which seems naturally to demand an examination and interpretation <u>of its contents as symbols</u>. Others among you, when asked to describe last night's dreams, would blush and refuse to say!

Part 2

From the variety of responses which we would hear to the question 'What did you dream about last night?', we begin to get an idea of the range of the activity. Research has shown that everyone, in normal health, spends part of the night dreaming. Remembering the dreams is, of course, a different matter. And just as there are many different types of dream so, we may suppose, do dreams have a variety of functions. Let us examine just five of many.

The first is that of the experience-monitoring dream. In this, the mind reviews past experience — the previous day's, or some event in the more distant past — as a way of learning the lesson of that experience. Often the dream has a consequence different from what actually happened, representing a more, or less, desirable course of action or outcome than the real event. After an unsuccessful interview for a job, I dreamed that I was in the same room, before the same people, but speaking this time calmly and persuasively. The conclusion to be drawn from the experience was underlined by the dream: that I should not become nervous and flustered in that particular situation.

If that dream had occurred before my interview, it would have been of the creative type. One important function of the dream is to help to solve problems by suggesting answers, or predicting difficulties and indicating a way round them. Another creative type dream is one in which the imagination operates in an unusually powerful and productive manner. Large parts of 'Dr Jekyll and Mr Hyde' came to the author Robert Louis Stevenson in dreams.

The dream function to which Freud and his followers attached greatest importance was that of wish-fulfilment. According to the great Viennese psychiatrist, in our dreams we satisfy desires which our circumstances, personal inhibitions, or the rules of the society in which we live, deny us the gratification, or even the conscious knowledge, of. It is my opinion that wish-fulfilment operates at several levels, of which the simplest require neither a complex nor symbolical explanation. An example of the simplest is a recurring dream which I had as a boy. The oldest of a large family, my parents could not afford to give me pocket money very often. In my dream I would be walking up the steep steps to our house. The steps were covered in autumn leaves, and as I climbed, my eye was caught by something shining among the leaves. I bent down, and saw that it was a coin. As I picked it up I saw several more partly covered by the leaves, and then notes, all of which I pushed into my pockets as fast as I could. I used to wake from this dream in a mood of great happiness. It was, alas, short-lived.

The fourth dream function is that which alerts us to some external reality, usually by some sensory stimulus: the dream of being at or in a fire from which we awake to find a cigarette smouldering in our bedside ash-tray. In this way the senses send messages to the 'sleeping' mind warning us of the need to awake in order to take some form of action.

Finally, the most controversial, the predictive function. Whether or not we believe in the possibility of events being predicted in dreams, the fact is that throughout the ages men have done so. Perhaps the most famous example, celebrated in Christianity and Islam alike, not to mention Judaism, is that of Joseph's interpretation of the dream of the Pharaoh of Egypt. When the ruler dreamed of seven fat cattle being eaten by seven thin, Joseph predicted that there would be seven years of plenty in the land, followed by seven years of famine, and that is what came to pass.

Part 3

Here are some descriptions of dreams, and some of the background against which they took place, for you to analyse and classify.

Dream A

I dreamed I was back in Finland, where I had once worked, standing beside a railway line which ran along the shore of a frozen lake. Snow was falling, and it was bitterly cold. In spite of stamping my feet and blowing into cupped hands I continued to get colder. I awoke to find that the quilt under which I had been sleeping had slipped to the floor, and I was, indeed, very cold.

Dream B
I was in a box at the opera. On stage, the leading bass was singing a solo, and as I looked at him I realised that the singer was myself, holding the audience spellbound by the power and beauty of my performance. In real life, and in spite of my early ambition, I can barely croak through more than four notes.

Dream C
When my grandmother was a young woman she dreamed of an older sister who was gravely ill, although my grandmother did not know it at the time. In her dream, she saw her sister being drawn from the earth, up through the clouds. The following morning a telegram arrived, announcing that her sister had died the previous night.

Dream D
I was uncertain as to how to lay out the garden of my new house. I had made a plan on paper, but I was not entirely happy with it. That night I dreamed of the garden at its best, in high summer. I realised that the layout was not as I had planned it. The next day I changed the plan to conform to what I had seen in my dream, and realised that it was in fact the best solution.

Dream E
I dreamed that I was crossing Whitehall, in London, behind two men who were speaking in a foreign tongue. For no logical reason, I decided that they must be spies. I woke up with that thought. You can imagine my surprise when I realised that a conversation in a foreign language was going on in my bedroom. I had fallen asleep with my radio on, and in the early hours of the morning it was picking up a transmission from a foreign station.

Unit 15   The World's Weather

Part 1
We are going to proceed from our brief consideration of the earth's surface and atmosphere to look at one of the basic factors in the planet's weather, the planetary wind system.

To reduce a complex system to one of simple proportions, the general direction of the wind flows over the surface of the earth may be summarised as follows; it is, of course, important to remember that when we talk of a wind, we name it by that part of the compass from which it blows. That is to say, a west wind is one blowing away from the west and towards the east.

Part 2
On a planetary scale, then, the prevailing winds in the mid-latitudes of both hemispheres are the westerlies. In the low latitudes on either side of the equator they are predominantly easterly — from the east — and traditionally known as the 'Trades', the name given to them by the sailors of old. The Trades of the northern hemisphere blow from the north-east, their counterparts on the other side of the line, from the southeast. In the high latitudes, although the trend is not so marked as in the others, the prevailing winds are generally held to be from the east, and are named the 'Polar Easterlies'.

Part 3
Let us now look, then, at a meridional cross-section of the atmosphere with these, and other, features marked on it. The cross-section represents a view of the earth's surface cut, as it were, from Pole to Pole, that is, along a meridian. The centre point, zero degrees, is the equator. Imagine that you are standing at the equator and looking along it. The northern hemisphere is in summer, to your left, the North Pole at ninety degrees north; the southern hemisphere is to your right, with the South Pole at ninety degrees south. The cross-sectional diagram depicts aspects of the wind system, and other features, with the northern hemisphere, I repeat, in summer, and the southern in winter.

On the vertical axis, height is measured in ten kilometre units, so that a vertical picture is given of the atmosphere from sea level to sixty kilometres. Our cross-section, then, includes all of the troposphere and stratosphere, and the lower half of the mesosphere.

You can see on the key above the diagram a list of features, some of which I want you to mark on it. There are the polar and tropical tropopauses, the stratopause, and the winds, the westerlies and the Trades, which are here referred to as the tropical Easterlies. They meet at the Inter-tropical Convergence Zone. You can also see the mesospheric winds, east and west, and the jet streams, which I shall explain shortly.

Well, let's begin to identify some of the features on our diagram. The stratopause is immediately recognisable. It's that straight line fifty kilometres high. The tropopause can't be represented by a straight line. Remember it's only eight kilometres high at the poles and twice that above the equator. The tropopause is shown by the continuous line, pole to pole. Note that it begins to rise towards the equator at about sixty degrees north and south. Above the equator, reaching about thirty degrees north and twenty degrees south we have the tropical

115

tropopause. In the polar regions, the polar tropopause stretches down as far as about sixty degrees north and forty degrees south.

I've already mentioned the mid-latitude westerlies. There they are on our diagram in the shape of these circular and wave-like forms stretching above and below the tropopause in mid-latitude north and south. The westerlies of both hemispheres are powered by the jet stream, bands of high speed winds found around the tropopause. Jet aircraft fly at this level, which explains why flying from east to west in mid-latitudes is more difficult than flying in the opposite direction, as the plane has to battle against the headwind of the jet stream and upper altitude winds. The jet streams are those circular shapes in the heart of the westerlies. Nor must we forget the jet stream of the Antarctic winter, the polar night jet stream of the upper, upper stratosphere.

In the tropical regions you observe the Trades, the tropical easterlies. They blow between thirty degrees north and ten degrees south. You can see them apparently emerging from the turbulent westerlies, running smoothly over these forty degrees of latitude. No doubt you remember that they blow from north-east and south-east in the northern and southern hemispheres respectively, and the area in which they meet, running from some eight degrees north to the same south of the equator, is the Inter-tropical Convergence Zone. There it is, represented by those two vertical lines reaching from sea level up to four or five kilometres. Finally, we have the east and west winds of the mesosphere, the mesospheric easterlies and the mesospheric westerlies. And so, you should now be able to identify most of the features on your diagram.

Unit 16   Heat Control & the Skin

Part 1

Because man is a warm-blooded animal, he can survive and function in a wide variety of climatic conditions. But this is only possible because he has a number of ways of adjusting the balance of heat in his body. Before looking at the human system of temperature regulation, we must see in general how body heat is gained and lost. By far the most important sorce of heat for the body is its own metabolism. Metabolism is the chemical process by which the body builds itself and uses energy. The energy comes, of course, from food. When the body works, heat is produced. This is why we get hot after exercise. Basically, the body is warm because the work it does produces energy in the form of heat. We also gain small quantities of heat by being in a hot environment, and by consuming hot food and drink we can add a tiny amount. Almost all the heat we lose is lost through the skin. We put out heat all the time in the form of infra-red radiation. We also lose some by conduction as we sit on, on a cold seat. The air round the body is warmed by it. This warm air rises and is replaced by cooler air. This movement is called convection and is the third way heat is lost through the skin.

Part II

One very important way of losing heat is through the evaporation of sweat from the surface of the skin. It is important because it is a process that can be finely controlled according to the body's needs. The temperature inside our bodies is kept almost constant. But the temperature of the skin and extremities varies a lot and is generally much lower than the internal temperature. Our skin is warmed by the blood passing through it. If a lot of blood is passing through, the skin is warm and, so, loses a lot of heat. If the blood vessels constrict — so very little blood is passing near the surface — the skin is cool and much less heat is lost. The blood flow in the skin is controlled partly from the brain, according to the body's heat needs. There is, if you like, a kind of thermostat. If this area of the brain emits strong signals, the blood vessels constrict, less blood flows, the skin temperature drops and less heat is lost. If, on the other hand, the brain puts out only weak signals, the vessels dilate, more blood flows in the skin, the skin temperature rises and more heat is lost. This is why people with pale skins go red when taking a hot bath — the body is trying to get rid of internal heat — or white when they get cold — the body is trying to conserve heat. The blood-flow through the skin and the mechanism for sweating act together to provide a very sensitive control system to make sure the internal parts of the body keep approximately the same temperature of thirty-seven degrees centigrade.

Part III

Many infections cause our body temperature to rise. This happens because the toxins, or poisons, produced by the bacteria or viruses alter the body's thermostat in the brain to a higher setting. So the brain signals to the body's surface that it must conserve heat, even though the internal temperature is normal. The blood vessels constrict and so you look pale and feel cold. You may start to shiver. This is one of the ways the body has of making heat, so your temperature rises even more. When the toxins begin to disappear from the system — when you start to recover from the infection — the thermostat in the brain returns to its normal setting. Because the body temperature is much too high, it operates the usual system for losing heat. The blood vessels dilate, you get your colour back and you start to sweat. Because the skin temperature is now high, you feel warm, So, oddly, with a fever, you tend to feel cold when your temperature is rising and warm when it is falling. Usually, a high temperature drops of its own accord but sometimes drugs are necessary to reduce it.

Aspirin does this. In very bad cases, or in very hot climate, it may be necessary to sponge the body with water to help control the fever.

Unit 17   Computers

Part 1
There are at present over one quarter of a million computers in the world. Basically, a computer is a device for storing and processing information, or data as it is called. People have found ways of doing these things for thousands of years, of course. But computers can process highly complex information at great speed. Because of this they are transforming many aspects of our lives. The development of microprocessors — you heard about their manufacture earlier — has speeded up this change even more. Microprocessors make it possible for computers to work much faster and to be made much smaller. So any particular computer can also be made more complex without taking up too much room. Computers are now being used in an enormous number of areas. We will look at a few of these. Computers are widely used in banking for processing cheques. The code numbers on cheques are printed in magnetic ink which can be read by a computer. When you pay in a cheque it is sent to a central clearing house where all the cheques are sorted according to the banks they belong to. Cheques for a particular bank are then sent back to it, where they are processed by another computer and the two accounts involved are debited and credited according to the amount of the cheque. Computers are also being used to process withdrawals and the payment of standing orders. Another development is known as the Electronic Funds Transfer. This system makes it possible to transfer money directly from one account to another via a computer. It is controlled by a computer in Belgium. If it is accepted by banks generally, this computer will become the centre of a highly efficient world-wide network.

Part 2
Computers are being used more and more in medicine too. The commonest, the commonest use is for keeping hospital patient records. There may be access to these at several points — wards, offices, laboratories and even operating theatres. Computers are also used in the delicate task of looking after patients in intensive care units and in monitoring those undergoing surgery. One of the latest developments is to use computers to assist diagnosis. A computer is programmed with information about a disease, using the accumulated knowledge of many specialists and text books. A doctor examining a patient may then be guided by the information given by the computer in what to look for and which questions to ask the patient. The information he gathers is fed into the computer. It may suggest further questions before finally providing a diagnosis. This kind of procedure causes some people anxiety. They feel it increases the gap in the personal relationship between doctor and patient. On the other hand, it makes widely available knowledge and expertise which before belonged to only a small number of specialists, or which had to be found with difficulty in published material.

Part 3
Computers are revolutionising the work of those who work with words. Up to now, in the production of newspapers, a reporter has typed his story, known as copy. This has then been passed on to the editor. After being edited, the story would often have to be retyped and then sent to the typesetter. Prints would then be made of individual articles and these, together with advertisements, would be assembled manually to form a complete page. This would then be the basis for the making of the printing plate. In computerised production, the reporter types his copy directly into the computer, which shows it on a visual display unit, or VDU. This is like a television screen. The editor accesses this story on his own VDU and changes it by typing instructions into the computer. Various articles are then arranged into columns according to a program run by the computer. The page layout is done on another VDU and the complete page passed automatically to the printing stage. For the office typist, things are changing too. They can now use word processors — small computers similar to those used by the reporters. If you make a mistake, you don't have to paint out the error before retyping. You just backspace and type the correct letter. The change is made on the VDU automatically. It is also possible to insert material — single words, lines or complete paragraphs. The computer itself reorganises the layout of the whole text to accommodate the changes. It can also store complete texts and organise the paragraphs as needed. This is especially helpful in legal work, where many standard paragraphs are used. When the text is completed, the typing of the page is again handled by the computer. You will realise from hearing about these uses of computers that there are big changes in the kind of work done by many people and, more important, in the number of people needed to do the work. The reading passage deals with the general problem of computers and employment.

Unit 18   Arthritis

Part 1
Your body has three sorts of joints; the first and second are those that don't move much, or do not move at all. There is little movement between pairs of vertebrae in your spine and none between the bones in your skull. The third sort of joint is the moveable kind. It can be a gliding joint, like the wrist or ankle,

117

a hinged one, like the elbow or knee, or a ball-and-socket, like the shoulder and hip, where one bone fits into the other one. Moveable joints have to do a lot of work and put up with great pressures and tensions, so they need to be very efficient and well-lubricated to reduce friction. The diagram shows how this happens in a typical moveable joint. At the end of each bone is a pad of cartilage. Cartilage is very smooth, tough and resilient. Around the joint is the synovial membrane or synovium. This produces a fluid which is used to lubricate the joint. The whole thing is enclosed in a capsule, which is made of fibrous tissue. This strengthens the joint. Mostly, our joints work very well, but all sorts of things can go wrong with them. Some are minor, some serious. Today we are going to look at two common and serious diseases of the moveable joints: osteoarthritis and rheumatoid arthritis.

Part 2
You all know that elderly people cannot move about as freely and easily as the young. They sometimes complain about pain in their joints and, if you look at their hands, the bones may look knobbly or distorted. The chances are that someone like this is suffering from osteoarthritis. This disease affects eighty to ninety per cent of those over sixty, so it looks at the moment that you will almost certainly get like this one day too. Osteoarthritis is brought about by general wear and tear over the years. Earlier injuries or possibly being overweight can, however, make things worse. What happens is that first, part of the cartilage is worn down and destroyed. In more advanced cases the whole cartilage breaks down. The bones then rub against each other. Extra bone grows around the edges in small lumps and it is this that can give arthritic joints a slightly bumpy appearance. The hip, knee or shoulder is the joint most often affected. There is stiffness and some pain, especially in the mornings, and often a rough, creaking sensation. There is no cure for osteoarthritis, though surgery is often used to good effect. This is a fascinating area of treatment but we cannot explore it now. In general, sufferers need a sensible mixture of rest and gentle exercise. Heat treatment gives comfort and aspirin gives relief from pain and helps control any inflammation.

Part 3
Rheumatoid arthritis is an acute illness which can cripple people at almost any age, though the first attack is commonest between the ages of thirty-five and forty. Like osteoarthritis, this type too is slightly more common in women. Also, it is found more often in the cooler parts of the world. The cause is not known for certain but there is evidence that it may result from a disturbance of the immune system, the body's defence against disease. In this case the body starts to destroy its own tissues rather than invading germs. What happens is that first the synovial membrane becomes inflamed and thickened; next, the cartilage becomes diseased and may finally break down completely. New connective tissue is produced around the joint, restricting or preventing movement. In severe cases, the ends of the bones become weak and brittle and break down. This is different from what happens in osteoarthritis, where the bone in fact tends to become thicker rather than thinner. An attack usually affects the small joints first, especially those of the fingers, and then moves on to affect larger joints. There is great pain, swelling, redness and fever. Rheumatoid arthritis cannot be cured and so the patient often gets recurrent attacks, with increasing ill-health and general weakness. Treatment given for osteoarthritis is useful in this disease too. Also, several drugs are now available to reduce inflammation and control pain. Cortisone has been used successfully too, but it can have serious side effects. Rheumatoid arthritis cannot be cured, but the situation today is much better than it was twenty years ago and research is adding a lot to our knowledge of the disease.

Unit 19 The World's Food

Part 1
Nowadays, more and more people realise that the world is moving into a critical period and whether we survive depends on how we deal with the crisis. One of the big issues is the world's food supply in relation to its growing population. As far as we can estimate, world population was almost stable at something under ten million for about a million years. The increase began with the development of agriculture eight to ten thousand years ago. After about seventeen hundred, when industrialisation began, the population started to grow at about two per cent a year. Today there are about four thousand million people and, if there are no major disasters, there'll be six thousand million in the year two thousand. A hundred years after that, there would, in theory, be anything up to sixteen thousand million. Even today there isn't enough food for everyone and, unless major changes occur, the situation is going to deteriorate rapidly.

Part 2
The supply of food is affected by many things. Some of these are obvious — things like the amount of land, water and labour available. Others have become more significant in recent times — such as the efficiency of artificial fertilizers. Other factors are more hidden but equally important. Food production and distribution involve the use of huge quantities of energy and we are facing an energy crisis too, since fossil fuel supplies will certainly run out in the next century. In addition, pests and pollution destroy parts of the food supply. Up to thirty-five per cent of world food

supplies are lost before harvesting as a result of pests, mainly insects, weeds and fungi. More food is lost after harvesting — as much as twenty per cent in some tropical areas — because of the action of micro-organisms, insects and rodents. Some of the hungriest parts of the world also have the most disease and this can mean food loss in a different way. People suffering from diseases like malaria and hookworm need up to twenty per cent more food just to fight the disease. Last, but not least, huge amounts of land are lost each year through urbanisation, road building and erosion.

Part 3

At present about a third of the population eat substantial quantities of meat. In terms of food use, this is highly inefficient as animal production uses up large quantities of vegetable protein which could be used directly by man. The average annual consumption of vegetable protein in poorer, vegetarian parts of the world is a hundred and eighty-two kilogrammes per person. In richer, meat-eating parts, each person consumes a hundred and fifteen kilogrammes of animal protein each year, but feeding the animals which are eaten uses up six hundred and five kilogrammes of vegetable protein per person. It is possible to increase the supply of animal protein by something like thirty per cent by the year two thousand. On the other hand, a much higher increase in vegetable protein is possible — an average for all forms of vegetable protein of about eighty per cent. Clearly, our survival is going to depend partly on the willingness of those in rich parts of the world to cut down a lot on meat eating and develop a more vegetarian diet. It will also, of course, be necessary to control population and, ultimately, those in the rich countries will have to accept a lower standard of living.

Unit 20   The Cinema

Part 1

The first moving pictures were developed in the eighteen nineties by W. K. L. Dickson, an Englishman working in the USA. He called his system the Kinetoscope. It wasn't the cinema as we know it at all. The pictures were very small and only one person at a time could watch. The earliest Kinetoscope used sound, separately recorded on a phonograph (an ancestor of the gramophone and record player). But there were many problems involved in getting the pictures and sound together, that is, synchronised. As a result the Kinetoscope was popularised in its silent form. The same principle was developed by the Frenchmen, Auguste and Louis Lumière. They called their system the Cinématographe and, between eighteen ninety-five and nineteen hundred, succeeded in exporting it to other parts of Europe, to India, Australia and Japan. The Cinématographe used a large screen, but the films were still very short — only about a minute long. Like the popularised Kinetoscope, it was a silent system.

Part 2

The early films were all made with fixed cameras. This greatly limited what could be achieved and made these early films more like the theatre than the modern cinema. So, an important advance was the use of a moving camera, which could turn from side to side and also move about to follow the action. *The Great Train Robbery* was the first important experiment in the use of a moving camera. It was made in nineteen three by Edwin Porter, an American, and lasted eight minutes. In the following years, films became much longer and the screens larger. Other refinements were introduced too but it was not until the early twenties that an effective sound system was developed. Lee de Forest, another American, found a way of photographing the sound waves which accompanied the action. This eliminated the major problem of sound/picture synchronisation. Although the first company to make talkies rather than silent movies used a system quite different from de Forest's, it was his which caught on generally and became the norm. An odd consequence of having sound was that, for a few years, the cameras once again had to be fixed. This was because they were sound-proofed to reduce the noise of their mechanism and the sound-proofing was so bulky that they could not easily be moved about. Once again, for a time, the cinema looked like the theatre.

Part 3

The last radical change in cinema was the development of colour. Coloured photography had been possible from the eighteen sixties, but early films were normally black and white and any colouring was painted on by hand — an expensive, slow and not very effective technique. In nineteen twenty-two the first real colour films were produced, using a two-colour system called Technicolor. It was quite common at that time to film whole sequences in one colour and the attempts to mix colours to get realistic effects were not very successful. In nineteen thirty-two Technicolor was improved by the use of three main colours and, broadly, the same system is used today. Colour took longer to be generally accepted than sound. It was expensive and people often felt, oddly, that it was less realistic than black and white. This was partly, of course, because the quality was not always very high and so the scenes could look very peculiar. Since the thirties there have been many improvements in the techniques of cinema and the style of acting has changed a good deal. But after fifty years the basics — moving pictures, colour and sound — are still the same.